The Short Book on the "Offer in Compromise," IRS Liens and Levies!

The Short Book on the "Offer in Compromise," IRS Liens and Levies!

Patrick M. Ryan, J.D., Ph.D.

iUniverse, Inc.
New York Lincoln Shanghai

The Short Book on the "Offer in Compromise," IRS Liens and Levies!

All Rights Reserved © 2004 by Patrick Ryan

No part of this book may be reproduced or transmitted in any form or by any means, graphic, electronic, or mechanical, including photocopying, recording, taping, or by any information storage retrieval system, without the written permission of the publisher.

iUniverse, Inc.

For information address:
iUniverse, Inc.
2021 Pine Lake Road, Suite 100
Lincoln, NE 68512
www.iuniverse.com

ISBN: 0-595-31683-2

Printed in the United States of America

Contents

The "Offer in Compromise" 1
Collection Information Statement (433-A) 9
Collection Information Statement (433-B) 16
Liens 21
Levies 23
Summary 25

The "Offer in Compromise"

Basically, what we do is send letters or postcards to taxpayers with tax liens. The purpose of our existence is to resolve tax liens, levies, and debt for taxpayers. We resolve anything concurrent with tax liens and debt. I would estimate eighty-five percent of our work is the "Offer in Compromise" (OIC) program. This is the best program the Internal Revenue Service (IRS) offers because, if a taxpayer qualifies for the OIC, the taxpayer stands to save the most money.

Our office also provides Installment Agreement, Penalty Abatement, and Innocent Spouse programs. With the Penalty Abatement, a taxpayer saves all accrued penalties and interest on the penalties. (I'll get to the Penalty Abatement later in this publication.)

Most of the work we do for clients is the OIC. The IRS makes the OIC available for taxpayers who have debt. You may see advertisements that read "Settle your debt with the IRS for pennies on the dollar." Well, there is a certain formula we have to use for the OIC. It's a pretty straight forward formula and most states do not use this formula because congressional law does not rein them in, as does the IRS.

The OIC formula—simply stated and the way I like to describe it—is "two sides of the same coin."

On the one side you have equity in/and assets. That is, whatever equity you have—whether it's liquid equity in a bank account or a life insurance policy, or equity in a home or an automobile—that's half of the taxpayer minimum offer to the IRS. The other half of the minimum offer is if a taxpayer has any monthly disposable income. This amount of income is multiplied by 48 months because the IRS uses a four-year period of collectability. So, if you have $100 disposable income per month, it's multiplied by 48 months. Now your minimum offer is $4800. If you have $1,000 in the bank, your minimum offer to the IRS is now $5800.

This formula holds true whether a taxpayer has an income level of $1500 a month or $6,000 a month. Usually, when a taxpayer has an income of more than $8,000 a month, it's hard to qualify them for the OIC program because the IRS uses National Standards.

For example, if a taxpayer pays a mortgage of $3,000 a month, the IRS National Standard level might be something like $1500 a month. Therefore, according to the IRS, the taxpayer has an additional $1500 of disposable income. You and I know the taxpayer really doesn't have this amount, but, under the IRS formula, you do. So that taxpayer may not qualify for an OIC. It really depends on how much debt the taxpayer owes, because $1500 times 48 months is a minimum offer of somewhere around $72,000. Now, if the taxpayer owes more than that, that's fine. But, let's go over the OIC in a little more detail. If you have any questions as you read along, write them down and e-mail them to me at patryan02@yahoo.com.

The OIC, offered by the IRS, is Federal Form 656. (See form section in back of publication). This form requires support documents ninety percent of the time. (There is a form where a taxpayer would not need supporting documents, but that's only for "Doubt as to Liability.")

The OIC has eleven sections. The first section is simply writing in your name and street address. There are two distinct Offers' in Compromise. One is a personal OIC and the other is a business OIC. To date, the IRS will not accept a combined personal and business OIC. There is a $150 application fee for each OIC. Many taxpayers have both personal and business tax debt. In this case, they would have to file two form 656's, two OICs and would pay a $150 fee with each form. Unless—under the poverty guidelines—the taxpayer is eligible for a waiver of that $150 fee. So, again, if it were a personal OIC, you would put your name, street address, city, state, and zip code. If it were a business OIC, you would not put in the taxpayer name unless the taxpayer name is part of the business name. You only put the business name and business address in section one.

In item number two, Form 656 asks for social security numbers. If it's a joint OIC, you write in the primary and secondary social security numbers. If you are filing singly, you only write the primary social security number. If it is a business OIC, you would leave item number two blank. Even though we know everyone has a social security number—including all business owners—item two is still left blank.

In item number three, Form 656 asks for an Employer Identification Number. If this is a business OIC, include your employer identification number. Most businesses—for tax purposes—have an employer identification number, although, some businesses do not require one. For instance, if you are a sole proprietor, you can simply use your social security number and tax identification number for the IRS.

I'm skipping item number four because item number four is a continuation of item number three. If you have more than one employer identification number to submit, then you would use item number four. But, in a case where you have two employer identification numbers, which is rare, but can happen means you have two distinct and separate business entities. Therefore, you need a separate form 656 for each business entity, and there is an additional $150 fee.

Item number five on Form 656 asks for the type of tax you owe. If it is a personal tax, check the box that reads "1040." Check the tax type and write in the tax years. For instance, if you check that you owe 1040 taxes, you'll write in the years 1997, 1998, etc.

Another form of personal tax is the Trust Fund Recovery Penalty (TFRP) which is a civil penalty. The Trust Fund Recovery Penalty should be included on a personal OIC 90 percent of the time. Ten percent of the time, it can be put on a business OIC without your OIC amended or having it returned to you by the IRS. Usually, the IRS won't return an OIC for that reason; they'll just ask you to amend it when they begin processing your OIC.

If you owe 1120 taxes, (corporate taxes), that should also be marked on the same line as the 1040, but the IRS will know to look for 1120 taxes if it's a business OIC with an employer identification number.

The 941 taxes are your employer quarterly taxes. You would choose this section of the form 656 if you had a business OIC. The employer 941 tax represents those tax monies the employer withholds from his or her employees for the purpose of turning the monies over to the United States government. When an employer subsequently doesn't turn over those funds to the government, but instead uses them to stay 'afloat', then that business owner owes business taxes. And, when you fill in those tax periods on Form 656, you will want to fill them in by quarters, not years. For instance, you would write down, 3/31/01 for the end of the first quarter of 2001, or 6/30/01, 9/30/01 and 12/31/01 respectively.

Also, if you are a businessperson with employees, you will owe an annual tax known as the 940 tax. This is your annual "unemployment" tax. These tax periods are also filled in using quarters, not years.

The Trust Fund Recovery Penalty is also, for the most part, cited by quarters, not years, although it sometimes can be cited in years. Any Trust Fund Recovery Penalty is a civil penalty. This penalty is assessed against anyone who was an officer of the company, owed a business tax debt, or had the ability to sign checks for the company. Even if it was someone named Mary who lived down the street and worked for the company for $10 an hour. If Mary had the ability to pay bills, she could conceivably become liable for hundreds of thousands of dollars of business liability.

She would, however, most likely be eligible for some form of tax relief, depending on her provable knowledge of the business operations. But she would, nonetheless be assessed a Trust Fund Recovery Penalty because she supposedly knew what was going on with the business, including the businesses failure to turn over to the government the monies withheld from their employees. And, Mary should have known—the government would contend—that she should not have paid other bills before paying the United States government. These types of taxes are marked under the Trust Fund Recovery Penalty section of Form 656 or under "Other" taxes as a civil penalty.

In item number six of Form 656, there are three reasons listed for doing an OIC. The first is "Doubt as to Liability." If you do a Doubt as to Liability OIC, you do not need to submit any supporting financial documentation.

Basically what you are saying is, "I do not owe this tax, therefore, I do not need to show the IRS how much money I make." It's simply, either the IRS believes I owe it or I don't owe it. Here, it is necessary to detail—in item number nine of the Form 656—your reasons why you don't owe this tax.

So, in item number six, Doubt as to Liability it might be a case where you are an Innocent Spouse. It might be a case where the IRS mixed up a social security number or where you only need to file amended returns because the IRS had previously filed substituted returns on your behalf. Or you might have a case where your bookkeeper or accountant counted some monies twice.

For instance, I've had cases where that has happened; a taxpayer went to the bank on a regular basis, withdrew money from the ATM machine, and placed it in his business account. The bookkeeper counted this money as a gain, not a loss. So, for whatever reason you think you don't owe the government money, like in Mary's situation—where you were blocked from or screened off from certain information concerning the day-to-day operations of the business—you would file under Doubt as to Liability.

The second reason a taxpayer can do an OIC is "Doubt as to Collectability." This accounts for about 95 percent of the way Offers in Compromise are submitted. Doubt as to Collectability means that the taxpayer has insufficient assets and income to pay the full amount of his or her tax debt. In these cases, it is necessary to support your Offer with the financial information Form 433-A if you are filing a personal or sole proprietor Offer.

Form 433-A, and Form 433-B, are necessary if you are filing as a partnership or corporation. In some instances a personal Form 433-A is not necessary for a business Offer.

Usually, however, if you own 100 percent of the business or a large portion of the business, the IRS will require a 433-A because a conversion from business taxes to a personal Trust Fund Recovery Penalty can be undertaken by the government if they sense any increase of collectability. (We'll go over Forms 433-A and 433-B in more detail later.) But basically, it gets back to the formula that we mentioned in the beginning. Your collectability is based on the combination of equity in/and assets and monthly disposable income multiplied by 48 months.

There is one other way you can file an OIC. That is under "Effective Tax Administration." Under Effective Tax Administration you are saying "I owe the amount the government says I owe and I have sufficient funds to pay the full amount, but, due to my current circumstances, requiring full payment would cause an economic hardship." This situation would apply to a disabled taxpayer living on a fixed income, but in the past, had money, and acquired assets.

Under this category, you need to make sure you have the income and/or assets to pay the full liability. For instance, if you owe $30,000 under the OIC formula, you need to show you have, at least, the ability to pay that $30,000, but it would create a hardship to make you do so. If your money comes from a pension or social security and this is your entire income, but you have a home that is paid in full and no mortgage, but are barely able to pay your bills. If you sold the home, sure, you could pay the IRS your tax debt, but you couldn't afford to pay rent because you are just making it on your monthly income.

This situation might also fall under what is call the "Delegation Order Number 11," wherein if you are retired and all you have is the roof over your head, the IRS will not consider the equity you have in your home.

For instance, I have had many clients who had insurance policies where the current cash value was around $15,000 and a home fully paid with equity of more than $250,000. Under the Delegation Order Number 11, the IRS will waive the equity in the home, but will take the life insurance equity of $15,000. You can use Delegation Order Number 11 under Doubt as to Collectability or Effective Tax Administration. Again, if you owed the IRS $100,000 under these circumstances, the $15,000 would pay your tax debt in full and if you had a lien on your $250,000 home, it would be released. (We'll talk about liens and levies later.)

Under Effective Tax Administration, if you owed $100,000 and you could pay only $15,000, then effective tax administration is the wrong way to go. But if you owed $15,000 and you could pay the $15,000, then the IRS also wouldn't take the equity in your home.

Item number seven on Form 656, is the amount you offer to pay the IRS. This amount should, at least, represent the minimum amount figured under the OIC formula. That is, the addition of your equity in assets and monthly disposable income multiplied by 48 months. Many, many taxpayers—I would say the fair majority of taxpayers—don't have disposable income. Therefore, their monthly disposable income times 48 months equals zero. Generally, most taxpayers only have an average monthly bank account balance. Whatever the bank account balance is, if it's $800 or a $1000, and nothing else—no investments and no equity in real estate or automobiles—then you would add that up, and that's the amount you would offer to pay.

There are basically three ways to offer to pay. The first is a cash offer, "I offer to pay $1,000, payable in a lump sum within 30 days after acceptance of my offer." You can also make it 60 or 90 days after acceptance of the offer. I see no benefit in choosing 30 or 60 days, so always mark 90 days. You can pay sooner if you are able. When does acceptance of an Offer arrive? You can typically expect a time frame of at least 12 months after submission because that's the way the OIC process is currently working.

Currently, there are two OIC Centers in the United States. One is in Memphis, Tennessee which handles all Offers from the West Coast, and the other is in Holtsville, New York, on Long Island, which handles all Offers from the East Coast. These centers handle all *personal* OICs. If you have a business OIC, your Offer may be processed at these centers or sent to an IRS location near your residence.

But, we would always mark the 90 day box for any lump sum Offer. Then, you have the option of paying via the Short-Term Deferred payment plan. Here, you offer to pay a certain amount, payable over 24 months. If you use a deferred Offer payment schedule, then, instead of using a 48 month collectability multiplier, you would use a 60 month disposable monthly income multiplier. The same is true for a Long-Term Deferred payment Offer. So, if you have $100 a month in disposable income, under the lump sum program, your ability to pay is $4800. Under the deferred, 24 months and up schedule, your ability to pay would be $6000.

Long-Term Deferred can be up to the amount of time remaining on the statute of limitations on the taxes you owe. There is a 10 year statute of limitations period on collections. If that statute of limitations is never extended, then it expires in 10 years. If the IRS has not collected from you or has not received a signed extension of the statute from you, then, at the end of 10 years, you no longer owe the IRS and taxes. If you had a lien on your home, it will be discharged.

The IRS likes to get extensions and there are certain things that extend the statute of limitations. Filing an OIC, for example, extends the statute of limitations.

As a rule of thumb, whenever collections are placed into abeyance, the statute of limitations is extended. When you file an OIC, the IRS no longer has the right to enforce collections. They cannot garnish your paycheck, freeze your bank account, or seize your property during the pendency of an Offer. In any case where collections are placed into abeyance, the statute of limitations is extended. If you filed an OIC and had two years remaining on your statute of limitations, and if at the end of one year your OIC fails, then you still have two years remaining on your statute of limitations.

The Long-Term Deferred payment option can last up to the life of the statute of limitations. And there is something else to be considered here. If you owe taxes for 1993, you would have filed in April of 1994. So, let's say you owe taxes for the years 1993 through 2002. You may still be able to qualify for up to a 15-year deferment on your Offer payments because you may be able to apply your payments to the oldest tax liability period. In this case, your oldest tax year liabilities will drop off first.

Many times, the IRS does not grant a deferred payment over the life of the statute because many taxpayers cannot follow through on the payments However, to many taxpayers, it's a Godsend.

For instance, I've had clients who owed the IRS $54,000. Under the OIC formula, it was determined they could pay $50,000, so they qualified for an OIC because of the $4,000 difference. If it was determined they could have paid the full amount, then they would not have been eligible for the OIC. But because they could pay $50,000 on a $54,000 tax debt, they were OIC eligible. Obviously, even though the IRS determines you have the ability to pay $50,000, you and I both know that is seldom the case. So, what those taxpayers did was pay $380 a month over the life of the statute, for a total of $50,000.

Now, some taxpayers may ask, "What benefit do I derive from hiring your service and having you get me a deal where I only save $4000?"

Well, these clients actually saved more than $4,000, because when they paid their tax debt on an OIC, there were no more penalties or interest tacked on. So, if it takes you five years or longer to pay your tax debt, say every five years, you're probably saving an additional amount representative of the amount you owed.

This particular taxpayer—paying $380 a month over the life of the statute on an OIC—saved at least an additional $50,000 or more in accrued interest and penalties. If this taxpayer were to pay under an Installment Agreement at a rate of $380 a month, he may never, ever get his debt paid. The taxpayer would die owing a tax debt. And, if the taxpayer was a homeowner, the IRS would look toward satisfaction of the debt through probate. So, the Long-Term Deferred option can still provide great savings.

If you are on an Installment Agreement plan when you file an OIC, the IRS rules dictate you continue to make your Installment Agreement monthly payment. This pretty much defeats the purpose of the OIC because if you qualify for a $1,000 Offer, why should you be paying $100 a month over 12 months while your OIC is processing. You would have already paid more than you qualified for and will not receive credit to your Offer. This rule is generally not enforced, but it's sometimes a better idea to have your OIC ready to go, and then stop your payments before you file your OIC.

Item number nine on Form 656 asks for an explanation of additional circumstances for consideration of your OIC. Use this section if you were doing a Doubt as to Liability OIC or an Effective Tax Administration OIC, or a Delegation Order Number 11 OIC. You are basically filling in responses like: "I am 65-years-old, on a fixed income, my health is deteriorating. I only have the roof over my head, and the only way I could pay my tax debt would be if I sold my home. However, if I sold my home, I could not afford to pay rent and would have no place to live, etc." Or, you may just write in, "I am applying for Delegation Order Number 11. I'm on a fixed income. Please don't consider my equity in real estate."

Item number 10 on Form 656 asks for a source of the funds. For instance, will you borrow from someone, etc? The IRS wants to know how you are going to get this money, because you are telling the IRS you don't have any money. Basically, the answer here is, "I will save money over time and/or borrow from friends and family."

Item number 11 on Form 656 is simply your signature and date. A spouse's signature should be provided where appropriate. For a business OIC, a representative of the business would sign and date.

That's pretty much it in a nutshell for Form 656 "The Offer in Compromise."

Collection Information Statement (433-A)

The mainstay financial forms for the IRS are Forms 433-A and 433-B. Both forms are Collection Information Statements. Form 433-A is for wage earners, self-employed individuals and sole proprietors. Form 433-B is for business partnerships and corporations.

We'll start with Form 433-A. It is fairly straightforward. In section one, you are asked for personal information. This is where you put your name, your spouse's full name, street address, city, state, and zip code. There is also a space for county of residence. County of residence is important because this is how the IRS determines a National Standard for housing in your area.

Many taxpayers think this reads "country" of residence and writes down USA. County of residence is important. For instance, take two different taxpayers living in California. They both pay $1500 a month for their mortgage but one lives in Los Angeles County and the other lives in Imperial County. The one in Los Angeles County may get full credit, while the taxpayer in Imperial County may be capped out under the National Standards at $1000. This is why county residence is important.

Next, Form 433-A asks for your telephone number and marital status. Martial status is important because it goes toward your National Standard, not only for housing, but also what you can claim as a monthly expense for food, clothing, and miscellaneous. This expense can be found on page six of the 433-A. (By the way, both Forms 433-A and 433-B have six pages each.)

If you mark married, you can generally claim a National Standard of two people or more. If separated, you can claim a National Standard of only one person, unless you are claiming dependents. There is actually an advantage to claiming only one person: a second person's income is not considered in your monthly income and expense formula.

Next, you are asked for your social security number and date of birth. These are pretty straightforward questions. Date of birth can be important to elderly taxpayers on a fixed income because these taxpayers may qualify for additional tax resolution considerations.

Item number six on Form 433-A asks for a list of dependents you are claiming. The more dependents you claim, the higher the National Standards will be.

Next, you are asked for employment information. Section two, line seven, is for those who are self-employed. It asks if you have an employer identification number. If you have an EIN, fill it in. If not, and you choose to use your social security number, simply write "N/A."

Next, you are asked if you have employees or account receivables. If you have employees, the IRS will look to see if you owe any business taxes. If you have account receivables, the IRS will look to determine extra future income. We, as tax law specialists, know how to set up account receivables to show that what you should receive in the future is nothing more than necessary operating expenses.

In section three, you are asked for your employer's name, address, city, state, and zip code. The IRS also wants to know your employer's telephone number, how long you have been with that employer, and your occupation, such as a sales representative, a plumber, etc.

Section four asks you to list any additional monthly income such as pension, social security, child support, rental, or alimony. You should always fill this in truthfully because there is no sense in keeping this information from your tax law specialist. This information is necessary for the tax law specialist to tailor the correct resolution for you. It's also important for you to know that the IRS has many databases at their disposal. They have databases for the Department of Motor Vehicles and real estate databases; they have databases that reveal the income you are receiving. Don't forget, usually, those who provide you with income, usually file this information with the IRS in order to lessen their own tax liability. So don't think you can get away without reporting your income.

Section five of Form 433-A asks for bank account information. This is the beginning of your list of equity because money in the bank represents equity. Simply fill in the bank's name and address, your account number, and your average monthly balance. Although the form asks for current account balance, the IRS will ask to see your last three months' statements to determine your average monthly balance.

Also under section five is a category for Investments. It is here you list any IRA's, 401k's, etc. You are asked to list the current value as well as any equity offsetting information, such as a loan amount or, if the account is used as collateral on a loan. Generally, you are allowed to subtract 12.5 percent of the current value for penalty fees. Usually, penalty fees are much higher than 12.5 percent, but the IRS also considers that over the next 48 months, you will gain back value lost to an early withdrawal. Many taxpayers contribute to these investments from a deduction from their paychecks.

The next item, line 14, asks for Cash on Hand. You should never put down more than $20 unless you have some exceptional situation going on.

Credit cards are next. Oddly enough, available credit is not really considered in your equity formula because in a sense, it's considered a double-edged sword. If you were to use credit to pay for your Offer, you would receive the benefit of additional expenses. The IRS generally does not allow for unsecured expenses, and it would be unfair for the government to place you in such a disadvantageous position.

Also in section five, line 16, of Form 433-A, you are asked to provide life insurance information. The IRS only wants to know about life insurance policies with a cash value. This excludes term life policies because they do not have a cash value. Term life is generally where you have a life insurance policy that when someone dies, you will receive money. This kind of policy has no current cash value so it should not be listed. Additionally, it is speculative when a person might die. If it is not within the IRS four-year period of collectability, it could not be counted as an asset.

Therefore, if you have term life, do not complete this section. Simply mark "N/A." However, it is very important to remember you can claim the amount you pay for your term life policy on the expense page. This will be important when we speak about beneficiaries.

If you have Whole-Life, you would fill in the name of the insurance company, your policy number, primary owner of the policy, and the current cash value, minus any offsetting outstanding loan. The value of the policy, minus and loan, is the equity amount used under the OIC formula.

Now, under section six, lines 17a through 17h, the IRS asks for Other Information. The first question is, "Are there any garnishments against you?" If you have a garnishment against your wages, you will get credit for this on your expenses. And, of course, the more expenses, the better for your Offer because you want to show the IRS you have no disposable monthly income. That's not to say that having a garnishment against you is good, but that's how we would report it as tax law specialists.

The IRS also wants to know if there are any judgments against you or if you are a party to a lawsuit. Being a party to a lawsuit can be advantageous or disadvantageous depending on whether you are a plaintiff or defendant. If you are a defendant and you stand to lose money, it's good in that you will be in a better position to resolve your tax debt.

Remember a basic rule of thumb here; when you are doing poorly financially, this is the best time to resolve your tax debt. Many taxpayers don't call for professional help to try and resolve their tax debt when they are doing poorly, thinking they will wait to make some money and then call. The best time to resolve your tax issue is when you are in financial difficulty. The more financial difficulty you have, the better chances you have to resolve your taxes. When you get back on your feet and start making money, it'll be harder to resolve your taxes for pennies on the dollar, or at least for less than what you owe. You'll probably be expected to pay the full amount.

So, if you are a plaintiff to a lawsuit, and you stand to receive a large sum of money as part of a judgment, this could possibly work to your disadvantage within the next four years.

The next question asks you if you have ever filed bankruptcy. If the answer is "yes," that's okay. The IRS simply wants to know the date bankruptcy was filed and the date it was discharged. The main reason this question is asked is because the IRS needs to know your bankruptcy has been discharged. You cannot, at the same time, file both an OIC and a bankruptcy.

The rationale behind this issue is that the IRS figures they do not have a true picture of your financial ability while in bankruptcy. For instance, if you're in a Chapter 13 payment plan bankruptcy, you may have $1000 in monthly bills, but the bankruptcy court is allowing you to pay only $500 a month for these bills and this is not a true indication of your expenses. And, if you're doing a Chapter 7 and you stand to discharge all your taxes, there is no sense in wasting the IRS's time in processing an OIC.

You can bankrupt personal taxes if more than three years have passed since the date of assessment. This is not three years from the date filed, but three years from the date assessed. For instance, you would have filed your 1993 taxes on April 15, 1994, but they may not have been assessed until October of 1994. Now, you can file a bankruptcy for business taxes and nine out of 10 times the bankruptcy trustee will declare all debts discharged. However, the IRS simply comes right back and declares you still owe these business taxes. The rule is you cannot discharge your business taxes in a bankruptcy.

The next question asks, "Did you transfer any asset for less that its true value within the last 10 years?" You needn't be afraid to answer any of these questions, but it's always good to let your tax law specialist see this, so he or she can make the best diagnosis for your particular situation. If you transferred an asset, take for instance, a home, it may be okay. It may be you needed the money to pay bills or the asset went through a forced sale for less than its true value. Here, the IRS is looking for transfers for the purpose of avoidance. For instance, if you transferred your house out of your name to your mother's name for less than full value and you still receive the benefit of living there rent free.

The next question is, "Do you anticipate any increase in household income in the next two years?" I don't really know, except in certain circumstances, how a taxpayer can anticipate this. If you're anticipating increased sales or finding a better job, you would still answer "No" because it is contingent, it is speculative. If you know for a fact that some bonus is coming your way or you have a contract that will provide for extra money, then you would need to mark "Yes."

Similarly, the next question asks, "Are you a beneficiary to a trust or estate?" If you are, then you need to mark "Yes." Most taxpayers are not beneficiaries of a trust or an estate and would even mark "No" if your mother has you in her will, where you stand to inherit when she dies. Again, it's speculative. Your mother could change her will or live for another 12 years, which exceeds the IRS four-year collectability guideline.

The final question under this section asks, "Are you a participant in a profit sharing plan?" If you are an employee, your pay stub probably indicates this, so you would mark "Yes" and include the value of the plan.

That brings us to purchased automobiles. The IRS wants to know the year, make, model, and mileage of your automobile. Many taxpayers are proud of their assets and when you ask the typical taxpayer how much an asset is worth to him or her—such as an automobile or home—they tend to over assess their value. Taxpayers do this because they are proud, as well they should be.

However, in this case, such pride would work to your disadvantage. What you want to do here is ask yourself, "If I were broke and destitute and needed money, and a willing buyer knowing my situation offered to buy my automobile or home, how much could I get?"

We're talking about automobiles, trucks and other licensed assets including RV's, boats, trailers, etc. So, you would write in the current value, the loan balance, name of the lender and the monthly payment amount. This, of course, is considered part of your equity to use under the OIC formula.

Next on Form 433-A, you are asked about leased automobiles and trucks, etc. Leased automobiles are good for tax resolution simply because you can never acquire equity in a leased automobile, but you do receive—as an expense—the amount of the monthly payment, up to a certain amount. I believe taxpayers are allowed $425 for the first car, and $340 for the second car in car payments, and an operating expense based on a National Standard that takes into account such things as insurance, fuel, repairs, etc.

Then we come to real estate. The IRS leaves room on the form for two pieces of real estate. You simply include your street address, city, state, zip code, and county. Fill in the date the property was purchased, the purchase price, and the current value. These are all important for the IRS to consider because, as we all know, property values have gone up in recent times. Then, write in your loan balance, the name of the lien holder, and the monthly payment. It will probably not bode well for you if you show the IRS you have more than one piece of property. If you do, you will not receive credit for the second property as an expense, but, as long as you are upside down on each property, you will not have any additional equity.

The following section deals with Personal Assets. Things like furniture, artwork, jewelry, and tools used in your business. Tools could mean books, computers, or hammers. You are allowed a $5,000 exemption for these items. Again, most taxpayers tend to over value these items. Keep in mind, if you went out today and bought $10,000 worth of new furniture, it would probably bring in only about $1500 at an auction tomorrow. The things that sell well at auctions are items like large screen televisions.

Section eight of Form 433-A asks for Account Receivables. Most wage earners do not have account receivables. Account receivables are monies owed to you from your course of business and have matured beyond 30 days. Account receivables are also important if you are in business and you have an account that you bill on a regular basis, when it comes to levies. (We'll talk about levies a little later.) If you are a sole proprietor, you probably would not have account receivables because payments would be made in a timely manner and may go toward necessary operating expenses.

This brings us to page six, the final page of Form 433-A Here you are asked—in pretty straightforward terms—your income and expense figures. Wages are always listed in the gross amount column because, over on the expense side, there is a line for taxes deducted from your paycheck. Business income is always listed in the net amount, that amount received after expenses. If you are self-employed, put down your net income. Also, on the income side of the ledger there is room for pension income, rental income, etc., that you must include.

On the expense side, food, clothing, and miscellaneous are listed at the top. This is generally for groceries, clothing, and other household items. You are allowed a certain amount per month, depending on whether you are single, married or have dependants. All these National Standards can be found by going to the www.irs.gov Web site.

We've already talked a little bit about housing and utilities. This line item includes your rent or mortgage, and any utility bills like gas, electricity, water, sewer, telephone, garbage, etc. The total combined amount goes in this line item. It will be up to the tax law specialist to see if that amount should be capped by a National Standard.

Transportation costs go on line 37. Add the full amount you pay in ownership costs and operating expenses, which include, gas, insurance, repairs, oil, etc. Again, your tax law specialist will resolve any National Standard cap.

Health care can include any amount you pay, not only for health insurance, but any ongoing treatment. This could include a co-payment or ongoing dental work, etc.

Taxes, listed on line 39, are pretty straightforward. Add the amount of taxes taken from your paycheck if you're an employee and if you're self-employed, the amount of your quarterly estimated payments.

Court ordered payments could include child support and any other judgement against you.

Child dependent care can include child support payments, but can also include things like special schooling or other kinds of special needs.

Life insurance can include term and whole life insurance policies.

Other secured debt means the debt is secured by some tangible item, like a washing machine you make payments on.

Other expenses can include professional fees—like for tax resolution—uniforms, periodicals, union dues and continuing education to improve your skills on the job. It does not include initial education, but if you already have a job and are told that a higher degree will earn you a better position, this tuition expense can be listed.

That about does it for Form 433-A. We'll discuss Form 433-B next.

Collection Information Statement (433-B)

Form 433-B is a Collection Information Statement used for business. If you are a partnership or a corporation, you would use this form. You may also fill this form out if you are a sole proprietor, but it's not necessary under the current IRS rules. And, it pretty much follows the format of the 433-A, with a couple of notable exceptions.

In section one, it asks for your business name, address, phone number, and employer identification number. It also asks whether you have a partnership or corporation, and the business you operate such as sales, construction, etc. The IRS wants a business contact name and address because any officer may sign this form as long as they have authority to do so.

In section two, Form 433-B asks for information concerning the individual responsible for depositing payroll taxes. This is the person most likely liable for 941 and 940 taxes. In this section, the taxpayer's personal social security number and home telephone number are required, as well as the percentage of the business owned by the person responsible for depositing payroll taxes.

Next is a section for all partners, officers, and major shareholders of the business. The IRS also requires they, too include both business and personal information, including social security numbers and the percentage of ownership.

Section three is Account Receivables. Generally, in a business, it is anticipated there will be many more account receivables which is more important to the OIC than for an individual. The OIC formula—on the business side—is the same as that on the personal side. Here, your tax law specialist can help you assimilate what the IRS should get and what it is not entitled to. The same holds true for business and personal account receivables; always look to structure your package to indicate that what goes out, and what comes in, is simply necessary operating expenses.

Section four is "Other Financial Information." The questions are similar on Form 433-A. For instance, "Are there any judgements against you? Have you ever filed a bankruptcy?" etc., are asked. When I use the word "you" here, I mean the business entity. For example, the IRS needs to know that you are not in a bankruptcy and why, if appropriate, was an asset transferred for less than full market value.

(The same principles apply to these questions on Form 433-A section six, lines 17 through 17h. If you have questions, please refer to this discussion on page ___.)

Section five, deals with purchased and leased automobiles. Again, the same principles apply. However, you would not list the same items already listed on 433-A. This will only provide a false doubling of your equity. These are only items purchased or leased by the company.

Real estate information is next. The same thing applies in that you would not duplicate what is already on the 433-A, but only those properties owned by the business entity itself.

Lines 11 through 11c, deal with business assets like machinery, equipment, and merchandise. Again, use the "quick sale" value, not the fair market value. Usually, quick sale value is 20 percent less than fair market value. This section also asks for any loan balances as an offset to equity you may show. Keep in mind that information concerning machinery, equipment, and merchandise wouldn't necessarily be considered equity in an asset because they are the inventory and tools necessary for the continued production of income, the continued operating expense for your business. For example, if you sold ice cream cones and have $100 worth of cones on hand, it wouldn't be considered having $100 in equity because every month you'd go through that $100 worth of cones to carry on your business.

Line 12 asks for investments. If you have investments like a certificate of deposit, etc., they should be listed here. Most companies do not have these kinds of investments unless they have a relationship with another company because all additional income is generally disbursed as profit. It is also important to know if there is a loan against your investment, or if your investment is used collateral, you can lessen equity.

Section six, lines 13 and 14, ask for bank accounts—checking, savings, and other. Again, don't duplicate information already contained on Form 433-A. Most businesses have a separate business account. Generally, this account is used for payroll and from time to time, has a high balance. You shouldn't worry about a high balance on any given day because the IRS is looking for an average monthly amount, after expenses—like payroll—have been deducted. It's the same idea as the ice cream cone theory—money goes in and money is taken out—all for necessary operating expenses. Therefore, you should not gain much extra equity here.

Next, Form 433-B asks about available credit. Most businesses have company credit cards apart from personal credit cards. The IRS asks for this credit information but again, it is not really considered equity because of the extra expenses it would provide for you.

Again, your cash on hand should not exceed $20.

This brings us to Income and Expense, page five. You are asked to choose a period of time such as 1/1/03 to 12/31/03 for the IRS to consider. Divide your figures by 12 to get the monthly income and expenses. Remember, the IRS will not consider any fiscal period more than six months old to determine your net business income.

Then you need to select which accounting method you use, such as cash or accrual. The rest is pretty self-explanatory and your tax law specialist can help you with questions. It is important to remember that whatever figure you arrive at after subtracting expenses from income, that figure should be the same figure on Form 433-A, line 27, "Net Business Income."

That's about it on the 433-B other than an additional section provided on page six for more account receivables. Remember: These 433 forms provide the basis of your OIC Form 656.

Let me explain a little bit to you about the OIC process. It is a linear or straight line process which starts when you file your Offer with the $150 application fee. Because of the backlog of OIC applications, it normally takes about three weeks to three months before first contact is made.

When the IRS contacts you, you will receive a letter from the OIC Group, and your representative—Power of Attorney—will be copied on the correspondence. The Power of Attorney form is Form 2848. (This form can be found in the back of this publication.) It's important to have a Power of Attorney form on file because you want your tax law specialist to know where you are with the OIC process. He can advise you with the next steps in the process and how you best can respond to requests.

Additionally, the IRS is obligated to call your representative, not yourself, with questions or information. The initial request from the IRS is two fold. If there was any problem with Form 656, the IRS will send you an amended form to sign. Generally, the IRS completes all sections on Form 656 as you originally had them, but sometimes they leave a section, like the OIC amount blank. Your representative can help you with any 656 questions.

Collection Information Statement (433-B)

The second part of the initial letter requests additional financial verification documents such as your last three month bank statements, paychecks, mortgage statements, etc. The IRS wants to verify those amounts against those listed on Forms 433-A and 433-B. If you listed $600 in monthly transportation expenses, then you need to supply the IRS with $600 worth of documentation. If you come up short, your expenses are lessened, but if you can show more, you will receive additional expenses. Either way, the amount of your Offer can be altered.

Any item requested, but not submitted, will be viewed as an intentional omission and your OIC will be returned to you without further processing. You must then resubmit your Offer with an additional $150 fee. If this happens more than once, the IRS may not accept your third try because they may deem your failure to submit all documents in a timely manner as an intent to delay or hinder collections. In this case, we can call the Taxpayer Advocate on your behalf.

So, submit all documents requested along with a cover letter to show you are complying with all requests. A cover letter is also helpful and can provide any additional information. Remember, the OIC Centers are backlogged and OIC Specialists are overworked, so don't give them any excuse to return your Offer.

Another important issue to remember at this critical juncture when submitting your OIC is to mail all documents in on time and request a return receipt, so you can verify the IRS received your document. Generally, the IRS will allow you up to 30 days to submit this information. (Sometimes it's less, but usually no more than 30 days.)

Extensions are hard to get. You can get an extension for a hardship. For instance, if you were in an accident and hospitalized, or if your mother was sick and you needed to care for her prohibiting you from operating your normal, everyday business, I would suggest you call the IRS—at the phone number listed at the top of the Financial Verification Request—about a day or two before the documents are due, and request an extension. Don't depend on an extension; however, so be diligent in gathering the documents and submit them on time.

Generally, after these documents are submitted, there is one more step in the process: the analysis. This can take about four months from the time you submit your documents depending on the current custom, practice, and backlog of the IRS Offer groups.

The IRS will then issue you and your representative an analysis, which includes an income/expense and equity/asset tables. This response will take one of three forms. The first possible response is "We accept your Offer for the amount stated on your Form 656." The second response is, "We cannot accept your Offer as provided, but if you increase your Offer to $XXXX, we will recommend acceptance." The third response is, "We have reviewed your Offer and cannot accept it because we feel you have the ability to full pay." If you receive this last response, do not be alarmed. It is not the end of your Offer, but the beginning of negotiations.

It is important to contact your representative to make sure he or she received this letter as well. Your representative will then advise you how to respond. Most representatives, like myself, will send a letter to the taxpayer, showing the client what information I need to respond and get a re-hearing on any disputed items.

Often you can negotiate with the Offer Specialist and, if that fails, you can appeal the Offer findings. However, you must respond within 30 days. If you do not respond within 30 days, you will lose all appeal rights. Your representative will have information from the Internal Revenue Manual that he or she can help you with and use to your advantage. So, don't give up or get discouraged if you get a letter saying your OIC was not accepted. This is the beginning of negotiations.

If your Offer is accepted, you must follow the OIC terms. This includes paying for your Offer on time and staying in compliance for the next five years.

This now brings us to a discussion of liens.

Liens

Generally, taxpayers become very concerned when they receive a letter from the IRS saying, "We are filing a lien against all of your personal property." Well, the minute you owe the IRS money, the IRS has an automatic lien on your property. It's a "silent" lien; however, and creditors will probably not know about the lien unless the lender or creditor does extra homework in finding it.

The IRS is unique in this regard because unlike any other entity you may owe money to, the lien is automatic. It's like an automatic judgment against you. For example, if you owe Sears or the hardware store down the street, before Sears or the hardware store can collect from you, they would first need to file a lawsuit to prove you owe them. This could take years to get a judgment if it goes to trial. A lien does not allow the IRS to seize or garnish; that's called a levy. A lien simply states you cannot sell property without first satisfying the IRS debt. It's like a passive collection tool. So, in essence, the IRS has a lien against everyone who owes them money.

Generally, the IRS won't perfect their lien unless you own real property. To perfect a silent lien, the IRS needs to send a representative to the County Recorder's Office. At this time, it becomes a speaking lien and creditors and lenders are made aware of the IRS lien. The IRS files in every county where real property is located in order to attach that property.

Liens work on a "first in time, first in right" basis. So, if you owe the bank a first mortgage, the IRS lien follows, but the bank is paid first before the IRS is entitled to monies. If you have a lien on your property and you sell that property, don't pocket any money before satisfying the IRS lien; that's considered tax fraud.

Keep in mind, when the IRS files with the County Recorder, they will send you a Notice of a Federal Tax Lien wherein you will have 30 days to appeal it from going into effect. To do this, you would file Form 12153, Request for a Collection Due Process Hearing. (See form in back of book).

If you file within 30 days, your request is forwarded to IRS Appeals and you will be contacted for your hearing. This process can generally delay the lien from taking effect for up to three months or more. Remember, all lien and levy hearings before IRS Appeals can be appealed to the U.S. Tax Court for judicial review. So you could get even longer, enough time to settle your debt wherein the lien is released anyway.

In nine out of ten cases, you will not prevail on your claim because the IRS is pretty good about giving you prior notice and an opportunity to be heard, and they don't usually mix up taxpayer identification numbers. Remember the reason you are filing for a hearing is to gain time and keep the levy from being seen by creditors, etc.

Why the appeal right is important is that you may have a collateral reason for not wanting the lien to show on your credit. For instance, if your business deals with government contracts, these contracts will be lost if you have a lien. We have, in these cases such as this, been able to keep IRS tax liens from appearing on a taxpayer or a taxpayer's business, until such time the taxpayer resolves his tax debt. Keep in mind that just because a tax lien is kept in abeyance, it does not mean you can sell property and pocket money. Because you are on notice of the pending lien, it would still be considered tax fraud. But, because you are appealing the lien, the IRS will place a code number on your account to show judicial activity. This code will extend the statute of limitations and stop all enforced collections on all tax periods involved in the appeal. There are a couple other things we, as tax professionals, can do for you if you receive a tax lien.

You may want to pay the IRS from proceeds of a re-finance or sale of real property to pay part, or all of your tax debt. We can do Lien Subordination's and Applications for Lien Discharge. Lien subordination is good in a situation where you can get money to finance your home. A lien subordination simply changes the positions of "first in time, first in right" so the lender may assume the IRS position. The IRS will work with you, if it's in their best interest—usually this is some kind of lump sum payment they wouldn't have normally received otherwise.

What if you were to sell your home and could realize $30,000 in equity, but your tax liability is $60,000? In this situation, the buyers would balk at assuming the lien on the property as well. A Lien Discharge works well to quell the buyers fear and remove the lien from the property.

Of course, if you pay your debt in full, or resolve your debt through an OIC, your lien is released in about three weeks. The IRS is very good about this and will not delay in releasing liens.

Levies

A levy is where the IRS, knows you owe them money, and they collect. They can collect by garnishing your wages or account receivables, seizing bank accounts or real property. So, levies are to be avoided at all costs. Oddly enough, most taxpayers don't seek the help of a tax professional unless and until they are levied.

Levies can be released and levies can be avoided. For the IRS to levy, they must've followed due process procedures of giving you notice and an opportunity to be heard. Usually, they send a series of letters reminding you of your tax debt, each asking you to contact them within 10 days. However, it is not until you receive the "Final Notice of Intent to Levy" with 30 days notice that you need to worry. You must file the same Form 12153 (used for liens as well) to exercise your appeal rights.

Again, this is a delay process to allow you time to resolve your tax debt. And, again, judicial review in U.S. Tax Court is available. Because you are appealing the levy, the IRS will place a code number on your account to show judicial activity. This code will extend the statute of limitations and stop all enforced collections on all tax periods involved in the appeal. You should have plenty of time to resolve your tax debt while this process is pending.

If the IRS has levied you, a levy release can be simple or difficult. In many instances, all it takes is a phone call. In more difficult cases, documents need to be submitted to show a hardship. If it's a bank levy, it's a one shot deal, and the IRS is only entitled to the money in your accounts at the time the levy is hit. If it's a garnishment, it is continuous until stopped. If it's on an account receivable you seldom use, it's a one shot deal. However, if the levy is on an account receivable you use often, it is continuous until released.

Banks need to hold your funds for 21 days before turning them over to the IRS. Usually, your tax professional can work out a release of levy to be sent to the bank before the 21 day time period expires. If you are levied by a revenue officer instead of the Automated Collection Service, a release may be a little more difficult.

Basically, there are three reasons to release or modify a levy. The first is to full pay your debt, which is usually not an available option. The second is to work out a deal with the revenue officer, and the third is to show a hardship. We normally show a hardship with past due notices or other showing of financial need for necessary living expenses. Remember: no levies can be issued during the pendency of an OIC. This is pursuant to the IRS Reform and Restructuring Act of 1998, which became effective January 1, 2000.

Your tax law specialist has many tools at his disposal to get you levy release, including going to the Taxpayer Advocate Service for 911 emergency assistance. If you have any questions or comments, direct them to patryan@yahoo.com or call 866-286-2241.

Summary

This is what Patrick M. Ryan, tax law specialist, can do for you:

- Analyze your tax situation

- Complete all paperwork required by the IRS

- Suspend IRS collections

- Submit the completed OIC to the IRS

- Give advice necessary to keep you in compliance

- Stop all penalties and interest

- Take your Power of Attorney so you no longer need to deal with the IRS

- Obtain an OIC Acceptance

- Perform your OIC Appeal—if necessary—for no additional cost

- To get started, call Pat Ryan at 866-286-2241 or e-mail patryan02@yahoo.com for a free interview and quote. Together we can get the IRS to forgive your entire debt for a settlement that is much less than what you owe! www.patrickmryan.us

Department of the Treasury
Internal Revenue Service

www.irs.gov

Form 656-A (Rev. 8-2003)
Catalog Number 28300X

Form 656-A

Offer in Compromise Application Fee Instructions and Certification

Use these instructions together with Form 656, *Offer in Compromise*.

This Offer in Compromise Application Fee package includes:

- Information you need to know about the application fee before submitting an offer in compromise,
- A worksheet that can be used to determine if you qualify for an exception to the application fee, and
- One copy of Form 656-A, *Income Certification for Offer in Compromise Application Fee*.

Note: You can get forms and publications by calling 1-800-829-1040 or 1-800-829-FORM, or by visiting your local Internal Revenue Service (IRS) office or our website at *www.irs.gov*.

What You Need to Know About the Application Fee Before Submitting an Offer In Compromise

What is an Offer In Compromise Application Fee?

When you submit an Offer In Compromise (OIC), the Internal Revenue Service expends resources evaluating your individual financial condition. The OIC application fee allows the Internal Revenue Service to recover a portion of the cost of processing your OIC.

How much is the fee?

The application fee is $150, payable by check or money order.

When is the fee due?

The application fee of $150 is due at the time you submit your OIC for consideration.

Do all OICs require this fee?

You must remit the application fee along with your Form 656, *Offer in Compromise*, unless:
(1) Your OIC is based solely on doubt as to liability (see Form 656, *Offer in Compromise*, page 1) or
(2) You certify that your total monthly income is at or below levels based on the poverty guidelines established by the U.S. Department of Health and Human Services (See *Offer In Compromise Application Fee Worksheet*).

The exception for taxpayers with incomes below these levels only applies to individuals; it does not apply to other entities such as corporations or partnerships.

How do I determine if I qualify for the exception?

To determine if you qualify for the exception, please complete the attached *Offer In Compromise Application Fee Worksheet*.

Is the application fee ever refunded?

If the Internal Revenue Service accepts your OIC based on effective tax administration or special circumstances (see Form 656, *Offer in Compromise*, pages 1 and 3, respectively), the fee will be applied against the amount of the offer, or refunded to you if you request.

What happens if I do not submit the application fee with my OIC Form 656?

Except for the two situations described above under "Do all OICs require this fee?" any OIC submitted without the fee will be returned to you without further consideration.

Where do I call if I have additional questions about OICs and the application fee?

If you have additional questions about an OIC or about the application fee, please call 1-800-829-1040.

Offer In Compromise Application Fee Worksheet

If your OIC is based solely on doubt as to liability, do not submit the fee. Otherwise, please complete the following checklist to determine if you qualify to have your OIC considered at this time.

		YES	NO
1.	Are you currently in bankruptcy?	☐	☐
2.	Do you have any unfiled federal tax returns for which you are liable? (You must file all federal tax returns for which you met the filing requirement prior to submitting your OIC.)	☐	☐
3.	If you are a business with employees, have you failed to make any required federal tax deposit for the current quarter and the two immediately preceding quarters?	☐	☐
4.	Did you use an outdated Form 656, *Offer In Compromise*, or outdated Form 433-A/-B, Collection Information Statement, to complete your OIC? (You must use Forms 656 and 433-A or 433-B, revision May 2001.)	☐	☐

If you answered YES to any of the questions above, STOP HERE. You are not eligible to have your OIC considered at this time.

The application fee does not apply to individuals whose income falls at or below levels based on poverty guidelines established by the U.S. Department of Health and Human Services (HHS) under authority of section 673(2) of the Omnibus Reconciliation Act of 1981 (95 Stat. 357, 511). The exception for taxpayers with incomes below these levels only applies to individuals; it does not apply to other entities such as corporations or partnerships.

If you are an individual, follow the steps below to determine if you must remit the application fee along with your Form 656, Offer in Compromise.

1. **Family Unit Size** _____. Enter the total number of dependents (including yourself and your spouse) listed in Section 1 of Form 433-A, *Collection Information Statement for Wage Earners and Self-Employed Individuals*.

2. **Total Income** _____. Enter the amount of your total monthly income from Section 9, Line 34 of the Form 433-A, *Collection Information Statement for Wage Earners and Self-Employed Individuals*.

3. Compare the information you entered in items 1 and 2, above, to the monthly Application Fee Income Exception Levels table below. Find the "Family Unit Size" equal to the number you entered in item 1. Next, find the column which represents where you reside (48 Contiguous States, DC ..., Hawaii or Alaska). Compare the "Total Income" you entered in item 2 to the number in the row and column that corresponds to your family unit size and residence. *For example, if you reside in one of the 48 contiguous states, and your family unit size from item 1 above is 4, and your total monthly income from item 2 above is $1500, then you are exempt from the fee because your income is less than the $1,667 guideline amount.*

2003-2005 Application Fee Income Exception Levels

Family Unit Size	48 Contiguous States, DC, US Possessions, Residents of Foreign Countries	Hawaii	Alaska
1	$833	$917	$1,000
2	$1,083	$1,250	$1,333
3	$1,333	$1,583	$1,667
4	$1,667	$1,833	$2,000
5	$1,917	$2,167	$2,333
6	$2,167	$2,500	$2,667
7	$2,417	$2,833	$3,000
8	$2,667	$3,083	$3,333
For each additional person, add	$333	$333	$417

SOURCE: *Based on 2002 HHS Poverty Guidelines, Federal Register, Vol. 67, No. 31, February 14, 2002, pp. 6931-6933, increased to account for 5% inflation through 2005, rounded up to the nearest $1,000.*

4. If the total income you entered in item 2 is **more** than the amount shown for your family unit size and residence in the monthly Application Fee Income Exception Levels table above, **you must send the $150 application fee with each OIC you submit.**

    Your check or money order should be made payable to the "**United States Treasury**" and attached to the front of your Form 656, *Offer In Compromise*. **Do Not Send Cash.** Send a separate application fee with each OIC; do not combine it with any other tax payments as this may delay processing of your OIC. Your OIC will be returned to you without further consideration if the application fee is not properly remitted, or if your check is returned for insufficient funds.

5. If the total income you entered in item 2 is **equal to or less than** the amount shown for your family unit size and residence in the table above, do not send the application fee. Sign and date Form 656-A, *Income Certification for Offer in Compromise Application Fee*, on the next page. Attach the certification and this worksheet to the front of your Form 656.

Form 656-A
Income Certification for
Offer in Compromise Application Fee

If you are not required to submit the fee based on your income level, you must complete this form and attach both it and the worksheet to the front of your Form 656.
(You should make a copy of this certification and worksheet for your records.)

Your name   SSN or EIN

Spouse's name   SSN or EIN

Signature Certification

I certify under penalty of perjury that I am not required to submit an offer in compromise application fee based on my family unit size and income.

Your signature   Date

Spouse's signature (if submitting a joint offer)   Date

NOTE: If the Internal Revenue Service determines that you were required to pay a fee, your offer in compromise will be returned without further consideration.

Department of the Treasury
Internal Revenue Service

www.irs.gov

Form 656-A (Rev. 8-2003)
Catalog Number 28300X

Collection Information Statement for Wage Earners and Self-Employed Individuals

Department of the Treasury
Internal Revenue Service

www.irs.gov

Form 433-A (Rev. 5-2001)
Catalog Number 20312N

Complete all entry spaces with the most current data available.
Important! Write "N/A" (not applicable) in spaces that do not apply. We may require additional information to support "N/A" entries.
Failure to complete all entry spaces may result in rejection or significant delay in the resolution of your account.

Section 1 — Personal Information

☐ Check this box when all spaces in Sect. 1 are filled in.

1. Full Name(s) ....
   Street Address ....
   City .... State .... Zip ....
   County of Residence ....
   How long at this address? ....

1a. Home Telephone (........) ....

Best Time To Call: .... am .... pm (Enter Hour)

2. Marital Status:
   ☐ Married   ☐ Separated
   ☐ Unmarried (single, divorced, widowed)

3. Your Social Security No. (SSN) ....
4. Spouse's Social Security No. ....

3a. Your Date of Birth (mm/dd/yyyy) ....
4a. Spouse's Date of Birth (mm/dd/yyyy) .....

5. ☐ Own Home   ☐ Rent   ☐ Other (specify, i.e. share rent, live with relative) ....

6. List the dependents you can claim on your tax return: (Attach sheet if more space is needed.)

First Name	Relationship	Age	Does this person live with you?	First Name	Relationship	Age	Does this person live with you?
			☐ No ☐ Yes				☐ No ☐ Yes
			☐ No ☐ Yes				☐ No ☐ Yes

Section 2 — Your Business Information

☐ Check this box when all spaces in Sect. 2 are filled in and attachments provided.

7. Are you or your spouse self-employed or operate a business? (Check "Yes" if either applies)
   ☐ No   ☐ Yes   If yes, provide the following information:

7a. Name of Business ....
7b. Street Address ....
    City .... State .... Zip ....

7c. Employer Identification No., if available : ....
7d. Do you have employees?   ☐ No ☐ Yes
7e. Do you have accounts/notes receivable?   ☐ No ☐ Yes
    If yes, please complete Section 6 on page 5.

ATTACHMENTS REQUIRED: Please include proof of self-employment income for the **prior 3 months** (e.g., invoices, commissions, sales records, income statement).

Section 3 — Employment Information

☐ Check this box when all spaces in Sect. 3 are filled in and attachments provided.

8. Your Employer ....
   Street Address ....
   City .... State .... Zip ....
   Work telephone no. (........) ....
   May we contact you at work?   ☐ No ☐ Yes
8a. How long with this employer? ....
8b. Occupation ....

9. Spouse's Employer ....
   Street Address ....
   City .... State .... Zip ....
   Work telephone no. (........) ....
   May we contact you at work?   ☐ No ☐ Yes
9a. How long with this employer? ....
9b. Occupation ....

ATTACHMENTS REQUIRED: Please provide proof of gross earnings and deductions for the past 3 months from each employer (e.g., pay stubs, earnings statements). If year-to-date information is available, send only 1 such statement as long as a **minimum of 3 months** is represented.

Section 4 — Other Income Information

☐ Check this box when all spaces in Sect. 4 are filled in and attachments provided.

10. Do you receive income from sources other than your own business or your employer? (Check all that apply.)
    ☐ Pension   ☐ Social Security   ☐ Other (specify, i.e. child support, alimony, rental) ....

ATTACHMENTS REQUIRED: Please provide proof of pension/social security/other income for the past 3 months from each payor, including any statements showing deductions. If year-to-date information is available, send only 1 such statement as long as a **minimum of 3 months** is represented.

Page 1 of 6

Section 5 begins on page 2 →
(Rev. 5-2001)

Collection Information Statement for Wage Earners and Self-Employed Individuals Form 433-A

Name _____ SSN _____

Section 5
Banking, Investment, Cash, Credit, and Life Insurance Information

Complete all entry spaces with the most current data available.

11. CHECKING ACCOUNTS. List all checking accounts. (If you need additional space, attach a separate sheet.)

Type of Account	Full Name of Bank, Savings & Loan, Credit Union or Financial Institution	Bank Routing No.	Bank Account No.	Current Account Balance
11a. Checking	Name _____ Street Address _____ City/State/Zip _____	_____	_____	$ _____
11b. Checking	Name _____ Street Address _____ City/State/Zip _____	_____	**11c. Total Checking Account Balances**	$ _____ $ _____

12. OTHER ACCOUNTS. List all accounts, including brokerage, savings, and money market, not listed on line 11.

Type of Account	Full Name of Bank, Savings & Loan, Credit Union or Financial Institution	Bank Routing No.	Bank Account No.	Current Account Balance
12a.	Name _____ Street Address _____ City/State/Zip _____	_____	_____	$ _____
12b.	Name _____ Street Address _____ City/State/Zip _____	_____	**12c. Total Other Account Balances**	$ _____ $ _____

ATTACHMENTS REQUIRED: Please include your current bank statements (checking, savings, money market, and brokerage accounts) for the past three months for all accounts.

13. INVESTMENTS. List all investment assets below. Include stocks, bonds, mutual funds, stock options, certificates of deposits, and retirement assets such as IRAs, Keogh, and 401(k) plans. (If you need additional space, attach a separate sheet.)

⌑ **Current Value:** Indicate the amount you could sell the asset for today.

Name of Company	Number of Shares / Units	⌑Current Value	Loan Amount	Used as collateral on loan?
13a. _____	_____	$ _____	$ _____	☐ No ☐ Yes
13b. _____	_____	_____	_____	☐ No ☐ Yes
13c. _____	_____	_____	_____	☐ No ☐ Yes
	13d. Total Investments	$ _____		

14. CASH ON HAND. Include any money that you have that is not in the bank.

14a. Total Cash on Hand $ _____

15. AVAILABLE CREDIT. List all lines of credit, including credit cards.

Full Name of Credit Institution	Credit Limit	Amount Owed	Available Credit
15a. Name _____ Street Address _____ City/State/Zip _____	_____	_____	$ _____
15b. Name _____ Street Address _____ City/State/Zip _____	_____	**15c. Total Credit Available**	$ _____ $ _____

Collection Information Statement for Wage Earners and Self-Employed Individuals   Form 433-A

Name _____   SSN _____

Section 5 continued

16. LIFE INSURANCE. Do you have life insurance with a cash value? ☐ No ☐ Yes
(Term Life insurance does not have a cash value.)
If yes:
16a. Name of Insurance Company ....
16b. Policy Number(s) ....
16c. Owner of Policy ....
16d. Current Cash Value $ ....   **16e.** Outstanding Loan Balance $ ....

Subtract "Outstanding Loan Balance" line 16e from "Current Cash Value" line 16d = 16f $ _____

ATTACHMENTS REQUIRED: Please include a statement from the life insurance companies that includes type and cash/loan value amounts. If currently borrowed against, include loan amount and date of loan.

☐ Check this box when all spaces in Sect. 5 are filled in and attachments provided.

Section 6 Other Information

17. OTHER INFORMATION. Respond to the following questions related to your financial condition: (Attach sheet if you need more space.)

17a. Are there any garnishments against your wages? ☐ No ☐ Yes
If yes, who is the creditor? .... Date creditor obtained judgement .... Amount of debt $ ....

17b. Are there any judgments against you? ☐ No ☐ Yes
If yes, who is the creditor? .... Date creditor obtained judgement .... Amount of debt $ ....

17c. Are you a party in a lawsuit? ☐ No ☐ Yes
If yes, amount of suit $ .... Possible completion date .... Subject matter of suit ....

17d. Did you ever file bankruptcy? ☐ No ☐ Yes
If yes, date filed .... Date discharged ....

17e. In the past 10 years did you transfer any assets out of your name for less than their actual value? ☐ No ☐ Yes
If yes, what asset? .... Value of asset at time of transfer $ ....
When was it transferred? .... To whom was it transferred? ....

17f. Do you anticipate any increase in household income in the next two years? ☐ No ☐ Yes
If yes, why will the income increase? .... (Attach sheet if you need more space.)
How much will it increase? $ ....

17g. Are you a beneficiary of a trust or an estate? ☐ No ☐ Yes
If yes, name of the trust or estate .... Anticipated amount to be received $ ....
When will the amount be received? ....

17h. Are you a participant in a profit sharing plan? ☐ No ☐ Yes
If yes, name of plan .... Value in plan $ ....

☐ Check this box when all spaces in Sect. 6 are filled in.

Section 7 Assets and Liabilities

18. PURCHASED AUTOMOBILES, TRUCKS AND OTHER LICENSED ASSETS. Include boats, RV's, motorcycles, trailers, etc.
(If you need additional space, attach a separate sheet.)

¤ **Current Value:** Indicate the amount you could sell the asset for today.

Description (Year, Make, Model, Mileage)	¤ Current Value	Current Loan Balance	Name of Lender	Purchase Date	Amount of Monthly Payment
18a. Year Make/Model Mileage	$	$			$
18b. Year Make/Model Mileage	$	$			$
18c. Year Make/Model Mileage	$	$			$

Section 7 continued on page 4 →
(Rev. 5-2001)

Collection Information Statement for Wage Earners and Self-Employed Individuals — Form 433-A

Name _____ SSN _____

Section 7 continued

19. **LEASED AUTOMOBILES, TRUCKS AND OTHER LICENSED ASSETS.** Include boats, RV's, motorcycles, trailers, etc. (If you need additional space, attach a separate sheet.)

Description (Year, Make, Model)	Lease Balance	Name and Address of Lessor	Lease Date	Amount of Monthly Payment
19a. Year Make/Model	$			$
19b. Year Make/Model	$			$

ATTACHMENTS REQUIRED: Please include your current statement from lender with monthly car payment amount and current balance of the loan for each vehicle purchased or leased.

20. **REAL ESTATE.** List all real estate you own. (If you need additional space, attach a separate sheet.)

Street Address, City, State, Zip, and County	Date Purchased	Purchase Price	¤ Current Value	Loan Balance	Name of Lender or Lien Holder	Amount of Monthly Payment	✱ Date of Final Payment
20a.		$	$	$		$	
20b.		$	$	$		$	

¤ **Current Value:** Indicate the amount you could sell the asset for today.

✱ **Date of Final Payment:** Enter the date the loan or lease will be fully paid.

ATTACHMENTS REQUIRED: Please include your current statement from lender with monthly payment amount and current balance for each piece of real estate owned.

21. **PERSONAL ASSETS.** List all Personal assets below. (If you need additional space, attach separate sheet.) *Furniture/Personal Effects* includes the total current market value of your household such as furniture and appliances. *Other Personal Assets* includes all artwork, jewelry, collections (coin/gun, etc.), antiques or other assets.

Description	¤ Current Value	Loan Balance	Name of Lender	Amount of Monthly Payment	✱ Date of Final Payment
21a. Furniture/Personal Effects	$	$		$	
Other: (List below)					
21b. Artwork	$	$		$	
21c. Jewelry					
21d.					
21e.					

22. **BUSINESS ASSETS.** List all business assets and encumbrances below, include Uniform Commercial Code (UCC) filings. (If you need additional space, attach a separate sheet.) *Tools used in Trade or Business* includes the basic tools or books used to conduct your business, excluding automobiles. *Other Business Assets* includes any other machinery, equipment, inventory or other assets.

Description	¤ Current Value	Loan Balance	Name of Lender	Amount of Monthly Payment	✱ Date of Final Payment
22a. Tools used in Trade/Business	$	$		$	
Other: (List below)					
22b. Machinery	$	$		$	
22c. Equipment					
22d.					
22e.					

☐ Check this box when all spaces in Sect. 7 are filled in and attachments provided.

Collection Information Statement for Wage Earners and Self-Employed Individuals — Form 433-A

Name _____ SSN _____

Section 8
Accounts/ Notes Receivable

Use only if needed.

☐ Check this box if Section 8 not needed.

23. ACCOUNTS/NOTES RECEIVABLE. List all accounts separately, including contracts awarded, but not started. (If you need additional space, attach a separate sheet.)

Description	Amount Due	Date Due	Age of Account
23a. Name _____ Street Address _____ City/State/Zip _____	$		☐ 0 - 30 days ☐ 30 - 60 days ☐ 60 - 90 days ☐ 90+ days
23b. Name _____ Street Address _____ City/State/Zip _____	$		☐ 0 - 30 days ☐ 30 - 60 days ☐ 60 - 90 days ☐ 90+ days
23c. Name _____ Street Address _____ City/State/Zip _____	$		☐ 0 - 30 days ☐ 30 - 60 days ☐ 60 - 90 days ☐ 90+ days
23d. Name _____ Street Address _____ City/State/Zip _____	$		☐ 0 - 30 days ☐ 30 - 60 days ☐ 60 - 90 days ☐ 90+ days
23e. Name _____ Street Address _____ City/State/Zip _____	$		☐ 0 - 30 days ☐ 30 - 60 days ☐ 60 - 90 days ☐ 90+ days
23f. Name _____ Street Address _____ City/State/Zip _____	$		☐ 0 - 30 days ☐ 30 - 60 days ☐ 60 - 90 days ☐ 90+ days
23g. Name _____ Street Address _____ City/State/Zip _____	$		☐ 0 - 30 days ☐ 30 - 60 days ☐ 60 - 90 days ☐ 90+ days
23h. Name _____ Street Address _____ City/State/Zip _____	$		☐ 0 - 30 days ☐ 30 - 60 days ☐ 60 - 90 days ☐ 90+ days
23i. Name _____ Street Address _____ City/State/Zip _____	$		☐ 0 - 30 days ☐ 30 - 60 days ☐ 60 - 90 days ☐ 90+ days
23j. Name _____ Street Address _____ City/State/Zip _____	$		☐ 0 - 30 days ☐ 30 - 60 days ☐ 60 - 90 days ☐ 90+ days
23k. Name _____ Street Address _____ City/State/Zip _____	$		☐ 0 - 30 days ☐ 30 - 60 days ☐ 60 - 90 days ☐ 90+ days
23l. Name _____ Street Address _____ City/State/Zip _____	$		☐ 0 - 30 days ☐ 30 - 60 days ☐ 60 - 90 days ☐ 90+ days

☐ Check this box when all spaces in Sect. 8 are filled in.

Add "Amount Due" from lines 23a through 23l = 23m $ _____

Section 9 begins on page 6 →

(Rev. 5-2001)

Collection Information Statement for Wage Earners and Self-Employed Individuals   **Form 433-A**

Name _____ SSN _____

Section 9	Total Income			Total Living Expenses	
Monthly Income and Expense Analysis	Source	Gross Monthly		Expense Items [4]	Actual Monthly
	24. Wages (Yourself) [1]	$		35. Food, Clothing and Misc. [5]	$
If only one spouse has a tax liability, but both have income, list the total household income and expenses.	25. Wages (Spouse) [1]			36. Housing and Utilities [6]	
	26. Interest - Dividends			37. Transportation [7]	
	27. Net Income from Business [2]			38. Health Care	
	28. Net Rental Income [3]			39. Taxes (Income and FICA)	
	29. Pension/Social Security (Yourself)			40. Court ordered payments	
	30. Pension/Social Security (Spouse)			41. Child/dependent care	
	31. Child Support			42. Life insurance	
	32. Alimony			43. Other secured debt	
	33. Other			44. Other expenses	
	34. Total Income	$		**45. Total Living Expenses**	$

[1] **Wages, salaries, pensions, and social security:** Enter your gross monthly wages and/or salaries. Do not deduct withholding or allotments you elect to take out of your pay, such as insurance payments, credit union deductions, car payments etc.
To calculate your gross monthly wages and/or salaries:
 If paid weekly - multiply weekly gross wages by 4.3. Example: $425.89 x 4.3 = $1,831.33
 If paid bi-weekly (every 2 weeks) - multiply bi-weekly gross wages by 2.17. Example: $972.45 x 2.17 = $2,110.22
 If paid semi-monthly (twice each month) - multiply semi-monthly gross wages by 2. Example: $856.23 x 2 = $1,712.46

[2] **Net Income from Business:** Enter your monthly net business income. This is the amount you earn after you pay ordinary and necessary monthly business expenses. This figure should relate to the yearly net profit from your Form 1040 Schedule C. If it is more or less than the previous year, you should attach an explanation. If your net business income is a loss, enter "0". Do not enter a negative number.

[3] **Net Rental Income:** Enter your monthly net rental income. This is the amount you earn after you pay ordinary and necessary monthly rental expenses. If your net rental income is a loss, enter "0". Do not enter a negative number.

[4] **Expenses not generally allowed:** We generally do not allow you to claim tuition for private schools, public or private college expenses, charitable contributions, voluntary retirement contributions, payments on unsecured debts such as credit card bills, cable television and other similar expenses. However, we may allow these expenses, if you can prove that they are necessary for the health and welfare of you or your family or for the production of income.

[5] **Food, Clothing and Misc.:** Total of clothing, food, housekeeping supplies and personal care products for one month.

[6] **Housing and Utilities:** For your principal residence: Total of rent or mortgage payment. Add the average monthly expenses for the following: property taxes, home owner's or renter's insurance, maintenance, dues, fees, and utilities. Utilities include gas, electricity, water, fuel, oil, other fuels, trash collection and telephone.

[7] **Transportation:** Total of lease or purchase payments, vehicle insurance, registration fees, normal maintenance, fuel, public transportation, parking and tolls for one month.

ATTACHMENTS REQUIRED: Please include:

- A copy of your last Form 1040 with all Schedules.
- Proof of all current expenses that you paid for the past 3 months, including utilities, rent, insurance, property taxes, etc.
- Proof of all non-business transportation expenses (e.g., car payments, lease payments, fuel, oil, insurance, parking, registration).
- Proof of payments for health care, including health insurance premiums, co-payments, and other out-of-pocket expenses, for the past 3 months.
- Copies of any court order requiring payment and proof of such payments (e.g., cancelled checks, money orders, earning statements showing such deductions) for the past 3 months.

☐ Check this box when all spaces in Sect. 9 are filled in and attachments provided.

☐ Check this box when all spaces in all sections are filled in and all attachments provided.

CAUTION *Failure to complete all entry spaces may result in rejection or significant delay in the resolution of your account.*

Certification: Under penalties of perjury, I declare that to the best of my knowledge and belief this statement of assets, liabilities, and other information is true, correct and complete.

_____   _____   _____
Your Signature   Spouse's Signature   Date

Collection Information Statement for Businesses

Department of the Treasury
Internal Revenue Service
www.irs.gov

Form 433-B (Rev. 5-2001)
Catalog Number 16649P

Complete all entry spaces with the most current data available.
Important! Write "N/A" (not applicable) in spaces that do not apply. We may require additional information to support "N/A" entries.
Failure to complete all entry spaces may result in rejection or significant delay in the resolution of your account.

Section 1 — Business Information

☐ Check this box when all spaces in Sect. 1 are filled in.

- **1a.** Business Name ....
  - Business Street Address ....
  - City .... State .... Zip ....
  - County ....
- **1b.** Business Telephone (..........)
- **2a.** Employer Identification No. (EIN) ....
- **2b.** Type of Entity (Check appropriate box below)
  - ☐ Partnership ☐ Corporation ☐ Other
- **2c.** Type of Business ....

- **3a.** Contact Name ....
- **3b.** Contact's Business Telephone (..........)
  - Extension ....
  - Best Time To Call ....am .... pm (Enter Hour)
- **3c.** Contact's Home Telephone (..........)
  - Best Time To Call ....am .... pm (Enter Hour)
- **3d.** Contact's Other Telephone (..........)
  - Telephone Type (i.e. fax, cellular, pager) ....
- **3e.** Contact's E-mail Address ....

Section 2 — Business Personnel and Contacts

☐ Check this box when all spaces in Sect. 2 are filled in.

4. PERSON RESPONSIBLE FOR DEPOSITING PAYROLL TAXES

- **4a.** Full Name .... Title ....
  - Home Street Address ....
  - City .... State .... Zip ....
  - Social Security Number ....
  - Home Telephone (..........)
  - Ownership Percentage & Shares or Interest ....

5. PARTNERS, OFFICERS, MAJOR SHAREHOLDERS, ETC.

- **5a.** Full Name .... Title ....
  - Home Street Address ....
  - City .... State .... Zip ....
  - Social Security Number ....
  - Home Telephone (..........)
  - Ownership Percentage & Shares or Interest ....

- **5b.** Full Name .... Title ....
  - Home Street Address ....
  - City .... State .... Zip ....
  - Social Security Number ....
  - Home Telephone (..........)
  - Ownership Percentage & Shares or Interest ....

- **5c.** Full Name .... Title ....
  - Home Street Address ....
  - City .... State .... Zip ....
  - Social Security Number ....
  - Home Telephone (..........)
  - Ownership Percentage & Shares or Interest ....

- **5d.** Full Name .... Title ....
  - Home Street Address ....
  - City .... State .... Zip ....
  - Social Security Number ....
  - Home Telephone (..........)
  - Ownership Percentage & Shares or Interest ....

Section 3 — Accounts/Notes Receivable

See page 6 for additional space, if needed

☐ Check this box when all spaces in Sect. 3 are filled in.

6. ACCOUNTS/NOTES RECEIVABLE. List all contracts separately, including contracts awarded, but not started.

	Description	Amount Due	Date Due	Age of Account
6a.	Name .... Street Address .... City/State/Zip	$	....	☐ 0 - 30 days ☐ 30 - 60 days ☐ 60 - 90 days ☐ 90+ days
6b.	Name .... Street Address .... City/State/Zip	$	....	☐ 0 - 30 days ☐ 30 - 60 days ☐ 60 - 90 days ☐ 90+ days

6a + 6b = 6c   **6c** $ ....

Amount from Page 6 +   **6p** ....

6q. Total Accounts/Notes Receivable = 6c + 6p = 6q $ ....

Section 4 begins on page 2 →
(Rev. 5-2001)

Collection Information Statement for Businesses Form 433-B

Business Name _____ EIN _____

Section 4
Other Financial Information

7. OTHER FINANCIAL INFORMATION. Respond to the following business financial questions.

7a. Does this business have other business relationships (e.g. subsidiary or parent, corporation, partnership, etc.)? ☐ No ☐ Yes
If yes, list related EIN _____ Additional EIN _____

7b. Does anyone (e.g. officer, stockholder, partner or employees) have an outstanding loan borrowed from the business? ☐ No ☐ Yes
If yes, amount of loan $ _____ Date of loan _____ Current balance $ _____

7c. Are there any judgments or liens against your business? ☐ No ☐ Yes
If yes, who is the creditor? _____ Date creditor obtained judgment/lien _____ Amount of debt $ _____

7d. Is your business a party in a lawsuit? ☐ No ☐ Yes
If yes, amount of suit $ _____ Possible completion date _____ Subject matter of suit _____

7e. Has your business ever filed bankruptcy? ☐ No ☐ Yes
If yes, date filed _____ Date discharged _____ Petition No. _____

7f. In the past 10 years have you transferred any assets from your business name for less than their actual value? ☐ No ☐ Yes
If yes, what asset? _____ Value of asset at time of transfer $ _____
When was it transferred? _____ To whom or where was it transferred? _____

7g. Do you anticipate any increase in business income (e.g. contracts bid but not yet awarded)? ☐ No ☐ Yes
If yes, why will the income increase? _____ (Attach sheet if you need additional space.)
How much will it increase? _____ When will the business income increase? _____

7h. Is your business a beneficiary of a trust, an estate or a life insurance policy? ☐ No ☐ Yes
If yes, name of the trust, estate or policy? _____ Anticipated amount to be received? _____
When will the amount be received? _____

☐ Check this box when all spaces in Sect. 4 are filled in.

Section 5
Business Assets

☒ **Current Value:** Indicate the amount you could sell the asset for today.

8. PURCHASED AUTOMOBILES, TRUCKS AND OTHER LICENSED ASSETS. Include boats, RV's, motorcycles, trailers, etc.
(If you need additional space, attach a separate sheet.)

Description (Year, Make, Model, Mileage)	☒ Current Value	Loan Balance	Name of Lender	Purchase Date	Amount of Monthly Payment
8a. Year _____ Make/Model _____ Mileage _____	$	$			$
8b. Year _____ Make/Model _____ Mileage _____	$	$			$
8c. Year _____ Make/Model _____ Mileage _____	$	$			$

9. LEASED AUTOMOBILES, TRUCKS AND OTHER LICENSED ASSETS. Include boats, RV's, motorcycles, trailers, etc.
(If you need additional space, attach a separate sheet.)

Description (Year, Make, Model)	Lease Balance	Name of Lessor	Lease Date	Amount of Monthly Payment
9a. Year _____ Make/Model _____	$			$
9b. Year _____ Make/Model _____	$			$

ATTACHMENTS REQUIRED: Please include your current statement from lender with monthly car payment amount and current balance of the loan for each vehicle purchased or leased.

Collection Information Statement for Businesses

Form 433-B

Business Name _____ EIN _____

Section 5 continued

10. REAL ESTATE. List all real estate owned by the business. (If you need additional space, attach a separate sheet.)

	Street Address, City, State, Zip, and County	Date Purchased	Purchase Price	¤ Current Value	Loan Balance	Name of Lender or Lien Holder	Amount of Monthly Payment	*Date of Final Payment
10a.			$	$	$		$	
10b.			$	$	$		$	

¤ Current Value: Indicate the amount you could sell the asset for today.

***Date of Final Payment:** Enter the date the loan or lease will be fully paid.

ATTACHMENTS REQUIRED: Please include your current statement from lender with monthly payment amount and current balance for each piece of real estate owned.

☐ Check this box if you are attaching a depreciation schedule for machinery/equipment in lieu of completing line 11.

11. BUSINESS ASSETS. List all business assets and encumbrances below, include Uniform Commercial Code (UCC) filings. (If you need additional space, attach a separate sheet.) Note: If attaching a depreciation schedule, the attachment must include all of the information requested below.

	Description	¤ Current Value	Loan Balance	Name of Lender	Amount of Monthly Payment	*Date of Final Payment
11a.	Machinery	$	$		$	
	Equipment					
	Merchandise					
	Other Assets: (List below)					
11b.		$	$		$	
11c.						

☐ Check this box when all spaces in Sect. 5 are filled in and attachments provided.

ATTACHMENTS REQUIRED: Please include your current statement from lender with monthly payment amount and current loan balance for assets listed which have an encumbrance.

Section 6
Investment, Banking and Cash Information

12. INVESTMENTS. List all investment assets below. Include stocks, bonds, mutual funds, stock options and certificates of deposits.

	Name of Company	Number of Shares / Units	¤ Current Value	Loan Amount	Used as collateral on loan?	
12a.			$	$	☐ No	☐ Yes
12b.					☐ No	☐ Yes
		12c. Total Investments	$			

Section 6 continued on page 4
(Rev. 5-2001)

Collection Information Statement for Businesses Form 433-B

Business Name _____ EIN _____

Section 6 continued

Complete all entry spaces with the most current data available.

13. BANK ACCOUNTS. List all checking and savings accounts. (If you need additional space, attach a separate sheet.)

Type of Account	Full Name of Bank, Savings & Loan, Credit Union or Financial Institution	Bank Routing No.	Bank Account No.	Current Account Balance
13a. Checking	Name _____ Street Address _____ City/State/Zip _____			$
13b. Checking	Name _____ Street Address _____ City/State/Zip _____			$
13c. Savings	Name _____ Street Address _____ City/State/Zip _____ ....13d. **Total Bank Account Balances**			$ $

ATTACHMENTS REQUIRED: Please include your current bank statements (checking and savings) for the past three months for all accounts.

14. OTHER ACCOUNTS. List all accounts including brokerage accounts, money market, additional checking and savings accounts not listed on line #13 and any other accounts not listed in this section.

Type of Account	Full Name of Bank, Savings & Loan, Credit Union or Financial Institution	Bank Routing No.	Bank Account No.	Current Account Balance
14a. _____	Name _____ Street Address _____ City/State/Zip _____			$
14b. _____	Name _____ Street Address _____ City/State/Zip _____ 14c. **Total Other Account Balances**			$ $

ATTACHMENTS REQUIRED: Please include your current bank statements (checking, savings, money market, and brokerage accounts) for the past three months for all accounts.

15. CASH ON HAND. Include any money that you have that is not in the bank.

15a. **Total Cash on Hand** $

16. AVAILABLE CREDIT. List all lines of credit, including credit cards.

Full Name of Credit Institution	Credit Limit	Amount Owed	Available Credit
16a. Name _____ Street Address _____ City/State/Zip _____			$
16b. Name _____ Street Address _____ City/State/Zip _____		16c. **Total Credit Available**	$ $

☐ Check this box when all spaces in Sect. 6 are filled in and attachments provided.

Section 7 begins on page 5 →

(Rev. 5-2001)

Collection Information Statement for Businesses Form 433-B

Business Name .... EIN ....

Section 7
Monthly Income and Expenses

17. The following information applies to income and expenses from your most recently filed Form 1120 or Form 1065.
Fiscal Year Period .... to ....

18. Accounting Method Used: ☐ Cash ☐ Accrual

Complete all entry spaces with the most current data available.

The information included on lines 19 through 39 should reconcile to your business federal tax return.

Total Income Source	Gross Monthly	*Total Expenses* Expense Items	Actual Monthly
19. Gross Receipts	$	27. Materials Purchased [1]	$
20. Gross Rental Income		28. Inventory Purchased [2]	
21. Interest		29. Gross Wages & Salaries	
22. Dividends		30. Rent	
Other Income (specify in lines 23-25)		31. Supplies [3]	
23.		32. Utilities / Telephone [4]	
24.		33. Vehicle Gasoline / Oil	
25.		34. Repairs & Maintenance	
(Add lines 19 through 25)		35. Insurance	
26. TOTAL INCOME	$	36. Current Taxes [5]	
		Other Expenses (include installment payments, specify in lines 37-38)	
		37.	
		38.	
		(Add lines 27 through 38)	
		39. TOTAL EXPENSES	$

[1] **Materials Purchased:** Materials are items directly related to the production of a product or service.

[2] **Inventory Purchased:** Goods bought for resale.

[3] **Supplies:** Supplies are items used in your business that are consumed or used up within one year, this could be the cost of books, office supplies, professional instruments, etc.

[4] **Utilities:** Utilities include gas, electricity, water, fuel, oil, other fuels, trash collection and telephone.

[5] **Current Taxes:** Real estate, state and local income tax, excise, franchise, occupational, personal property, sales and the employer's portion of employment taxes.

☐ Check this box when all spaces in Sect. 7 are filled in.

☐ Check this box when all spaces in all sections are filled in and all attachments provided.

⚠ **CAUTION** *Failure to complete all entry spaces may result in rejection or significant delay in the resolution of your account.*

Certification: Under penalties of perjury, I declare that to the best of my knowledge and belief this statement of assets, liabilities, and other information is true, correct and complete.

....
Print Name Title

✎ ....
Your Signature Date

Collection Information Statement for Businesses Form 433-B

Business Name .... EIN ....

Section 3 Accounts/ Notes Receivable continued	ACCOUNTS/NOTES RECEIVABLE CONTINUATION PAGE. List all contracts separately, including contracts awarded, but not started. (If you need additional space, copy this page and attach to the 433-B package.)			
	Description	Amount Due	Date Due	Age of Account
Use only if needed.	6d. Name .... Street Address .... City/State/Zip	$		☐ 0 - 30 days ☐ 30 - 60 days ☐ 60 - 90 days ☐ 90+ days
☐ Check this box if this page is not needed.	6e. Name .... Street Address .... City/State/Zip	$		☐ 0 - 30 days ☐ 30 - 60 days ☐ 60 - 90 days ☐ 90+ days
	6f. Name .... Street Address .... City/State/Zip	$		☐ 0 - 30 days ☐ 30 - 60 days ☐ 60 - 90 days ☐ 90+ days
	6g. Name .... Street Address .... City/State/Zip	$		☐ 0 - 30 days ☐ 30 - 60 days ☐ 60 - 90 days ☐ 90+ days
	6h. Name .... Street Address .... City/State/Zip	$		☐ 0 - 30 days ☐ 30 - 60 days ☐ 60 - 90 days ☐ 90+ days
	6i. Name .... Street Address .... City/State/Zip	$		☐ 0 - 30 days ☐ 30 - 60 days ☐ 60 - 90 days ☐ 90+ days
	6j. Name .... Street Address .... City/State/Zip	$		☐ 0 - 30 days ☐ 30 - 60 days ☐ 60 - 90 days ☐ 90+ days
	6k. Name .... Street Address .... City/State/Zip	$		☐ 0 - 30 days ☐ 30 - 60 days ☐ 60 - 90 days ☐ 90+ days
	6l. Name .... Street Address .... City/State/Zip	$		☐ 0 - 30 days ☐ 30 - 60 days ☐ 60 - 90 days ☐ 90+ days
	6m. Name .... Street Address .... City/State/Zip	$		☐ 0 - 30 days ☐ 30 - 60 days ☐ 60 - 90 days ☐ 90+ days
	6n. Name .... Street Address .... City/State/Zip	$		☐ 0 - 30 days ☐ 30 - 60 days ☐ 60 - 90 days ☐ 90+ days
	6o. Name .... Street Address .... City/State/Zip	$		☐ 0 - 30 days ☐ 30 - 60 days ☐ 60 - 90 days ☐ 90+ days
☐ Check this box when all spaces in Sect. 3 are filled in.	Add lines 6d through 6o = 6p $		*(Add this amount to amount on line 6c, Section 3, page 1)*	

(Rev. 5-2001)

OMB No. 1545-1504

Department of the Treasury – Internal Revenue Service

TAXPAYER ADVOCATE SERVICE

Application for Taxpayer Assistance Order (ATAO)

Form **911** (Rev. 3-2000)

Section I. — Taxpayer Information

1. Name(s) as shown on tax return

2. Current mailing address (Number, Street & Apartment Number)

3. City, Town or Post Office, State and ZIP Code

4. Your Social Security Number

5. Social Security No. of Spouse

6. Tax Form(s)

7. Tax Period(s)

8. Employer Identification Number (if applicable)

9. E-Mail address

10. Fax number

11. Person to contact

12. Daytime telephone number

13. Best time to call

14. Please describe the problem and the significant hardship it is creating. *(If more space is needed, attach additional sheets.)*

15. Please describe the relief you are requesting. *(If more space is needed, attach additional sheets.)*

I understand that Taxpayer Advocate employees may contact third parties in order to respond to this request and I authorize such contacts to be made. Further, by authorizing the Taxpayer Advocate Service to contact third parties, I understand that I will not receive notice, pursuant to section 7602(c) of the Internal Revenue Code, of third parties contacted in connection with this request.

16. Signature of taxpayer or corporate officer

17. Date

18. Signature of spouse

19. Date

Section II. — Representative Information (if applicable)

1. Name of Authorized Representative

2. Mailing Address

3. Centralized Authorization File Number (CAF)

4. Daytime telephone number

5. Fax number

6. Signature of Representative

7. Date

Cat. No. 16965S

Form **911** (Rev. 3-2000)

Section III. (For Internal Revenue Service only)

Taxpayer Name	Taxpayer Identification Number (TIN)		
1. Name of Initiating Employee	2. Employee Telephone Number	3. Operating Division or Function	4. Office
		6. IRS Received Date	

5. How Identified & Received (Check the appropriate box)

IRS Function Identified Issue as Meeting TAS Criteria
- ❏ (r) Functional referral (Functional area identified TP/Rep issue as meeting TAS criteria)
- ❏ (x) Congressional correspondence/inquiry not addressed to TAS but referred for TAS handling

Taxpayer or Representative Requested TAS Assistance
- ❏ (c) Taxpayer or representative filed Form 911 or sent other correspondence to TAS
- ❏ (n) Taxpayer or representative called into a National Taxpayer Advocate (NTA) Toll-Free site
- ❏ (p) Taxpayer or representative called TAS (other than NTA Toll-Free)
- ❏ (s) Functional referral (Taxpayer or representative specifically requested TAS assistance)
- ❏ (w) Taxpayer or representative sought TAS assistance in a TAS walk-in area
- ❏ (y) Congressional corresp/inquiry addressed to TAS or any Congressional specifically requesting TAS assistance

7. TAS Criteria (Check the appropriate box)
- ❏ (1) Taxpayer is suffering or about to suffer a significant hardship
- ❏ (2) Taxpayer is facing an immediate threat of adverse action
- ❏ (3) Taxpayer will incur significant costs, including fees for professional representation, if relief is not granted
- ❏ (4) Taxpayer will suffer irreparable injury or long-term adverse impact if relief is not granted
- ❏ (5) Taxpayer experienced an IRS delay of more than 30 calendar days in resolving an account-related problem or inquiry
- ❏ (6) Taxpayer did not receive a response or resolution to their problem by the date promised
- ❏ (7) A system or procedure has either failed to operate as intended or failed to resolve a taxpayer problem or dispute with the IRS
- ❏ (8) Congressional Duplicate of any criteria or non-criteria case already in TAS or on TAMIS
- ❏ (9) Any issue/problem not meeting the above TAS criteria but kept in TAS for handling and resolution

8. Initiating Employee: What actions did you take to help resolve the problem?

9. Initiating Employee: State reason(s) why relief was not provided.

Section III Instructions (For Internal Revenue Service only)
1. Enter your name.
2. Enter your telephone number.
3. Enter your function (i.e.: ACS, Collection, Examination, Customer Service, etc.). If you are now part of one of the new Business Operating Divisions (Wage & Investment Income, Small Business/Self-Employed, Large/Mid-Size Business, Tax-Exempt/Govt Entity), enter the name of the division.
4. Enter the number/Organization Code for your office. (e.g., 18 for AUSC, 95 for Los Angeles).
5. Check the appropriate box that best reflects how the taxpayer informed us of the problem. For example, did TP call or write an IRS function or TAS? Did TP specifically request TAS assistance/handling or did the function identify the issue as meeting TAS criteria?
6. The IRS Received Date is the date TP/Rep first informed the IRS of the problem. Enter the date the TP/Rep first called, walked in or wrote the IRS to seek assistance with getting the problem resolved.
7. Check the box that best describes the reason/justification for Taxpayer Advocate Service (TAS) assistance and handling.
8. Indicate the actions you took to help resolve taxpayer's problem.
9. State the reason(s) that prevented you from resolving taxpayer's problem and from providing relief. For example, levy proceeds cannot be returned since they were already applied to a valid liability; an overpayment cannot be refunded since the refund statute expired; or current law precludes a specific interest abatement.

Section IV. (For Taxpayer Advocate Service only)

1. TAMIS CF#	2. BOD/Client	3. How Recd Code	4. Criteria Code	5. IRS Recd Date	6. TAS Recd Date
7. Reopen Ind	8. Func/Unit Assigned	9. Employee Assigned	10. Major Issue Code	11. ATAO Code/Subcode	12. PSD Code
13. Special Case Code	14. Complexity Code	15. Outreach	16. Local Use Code ❏ TP |_|_|_|_| ❏ Case |_|	17. Relief Date	18. TAS Clsd Date
19. Cust Satisfact Cde	20. Root Cause Code				

Hardship ❏ Yes ❏ No	Taxpayer Advocate Signature	Date

Cat. No. 16965S

Form **911** (Rev. 3-2000)

Instructions

When to use this form: Use this form to request relief if any of the following apply to you:
1. You are suffering or about to suffer a significant hardship;
2. You are facing an immediate threat of adverse action;
3. You will incur significant costs, including fees for professional representation, if relief is not granted;
4. You will suffer irreparable injury or long-term adverse impact if relief is not granted;
5. You experienced an IRS delay of more than 30 calendar days in resolving an account-related problem or inquiry;
6. You did not receive a response or resolution to your problem by the date promised;
7. A system or procedure has either failed to operate as intended or failed to resolve your problem or dispute with the IRS.

If an IRS office will not grant the relief requested or will not grant the relief in time to avoid the significant hardship, you may submit this form. No enforcement action will be taken while we are reviewing your application.

Where to Submit This Form: Submit this application to the Taxpayer Advocate office located in the state or city where you reside. For the address of the Taxpayer Advocate in your state or city or for additional information call the National Taxpayer Advocate Toll-Free Number 1-877-777-4778.

Third Party Contact: You should understand that in order to respond to this request you are also authorizing the Taxpayer Advocate Service to contact third parties when necessary and that you will not receive further notice regarding contacted parties. See IRC 7602(c).

Overseas Taxpayers: Taxpayers residing overseas can submit this application by mail to the Taxpayer Advocate, Internal Revenue Service, PO Box 193479, San Juan, Puerto Rico 00919 or in person at 2 Ponce de Leon Avenue, Mercantil Plaza Building, Room GF05A, Hato Rey PR 00918. The application can also be faxed to (787) 759-4535.

Caution: Incomplete applications or applications submitted to an Advocate office outside of your geographical location may result in delays. If you do not hear from us within one week of submitting Form 911, please contact the Taxpayer Advocate office where you originally submitted your application.

Section I Instructions--Taxpayer Information

1. Enter your name(s) as shown on the tax return that relates to this application for relief.
2. Enter your current mailing address, including street number and name and apartment number.
3. Enter your city, town or post office, state and ZIP code.
4. Enter your Social Security Number.
5. Enter the Social Security Number of your spouse if this application relates to a jointly filed return.
6. Enter the number of the Federal tax return or form that relates to this application. For example, an individual taxpayer with an income tax issue would enter Form 1040.
7. Enter the quarterly, annual or other tax period that relates to this application. For example, if this request involves an income tax issue, enter the calendar or fiscal year; if an employment tax issue, enter the calendar quarter.
8. Enter your Employer Identification Number if this relief request involves a business or non-individual entity (e.g., a partnership, corporation, trust, self-employed individual with employees).
9. Enter your E-mail address.
10. Enter your fax number including the area code.
11. Enter the name of the individual we should contact. For partnerships, corporations, trusts, etc., enter the name of the individual authorized to act on the entity's behalf.
12. Enter your daytime telephone number including the area code.
13. Indicate the best time to call you. Please specify a.m. or p.m. hours.
14. Describe the problem and the significant hardship it is creating for you. Specify the actions that the IRS has taken (or not taken) to cause the problem and ensuing hardship. **If the problem involves an IRS delay of more than 30 days in resolving your issue, indicate the date you first contacted the IRS for assistance in resolving your problem.**
15. Describe the relief you are seeking. Specify the actions that you want taken and that you believe necessary to relieve the significant hardship. Furnish if applicable any relevant proof and corroboration as to why relief is warranted or why you cannot or should not meet current IRS demands to satisfy your tax obligations.
16.&18. If this application is a joint relief request relating to a joint tax liability, both spouses should sign in the appropriate blocks. If only one spouse is requesting relief relating to a joint tax liability, only the requesting spouse has to sign the application. If this application is being submitted for another individual, only a person authorized and empowered to act on that individual's behalf should sign the application.
    NOTE: The signing of this application allows the IRS by law to suspend, for the period of time it takes the Advocate to review and decide upon your request, any applicable statutory periods of limitation relating to the assessment or collection of taxes..
17.&19. Enter the date the application was signed.

Section II Instructions--Representative Information

Taxpayers: If you wish to have a representative act on your behalf, you must give him/her power of attorney or tax information authorization for the tax return(s) and period(s) involved. For additional information see Form 2848, Power of Attorney and Declaration of Representative or Form 8821, Tax Information Authorization, and the accompanying instructions.

Representatives: If you are an authorized representative submitting this request on behalf of the taxpayer identified in Section I, complete Blocks 1 through 7 of Section II. Attach a copy of Form 2848, Form 8821 or other power of attorney. Enter your Centralized Authorization File (CAF) number in Block 3 of Section II. The CAF number is the unique number that the IRS assigns to a representative after Form 2848 or Form 8821 is filed with an IRS office.

Paperwork Reduction Act Notice: We ask for the information on this form to carry out the Internal Revenue laws of the United States. Your response is voluntary. You are not required to provide the information requested on a form that is subject to the Paperwork Reduction Act unless the form displays a valid OMB control number. Books or records relating to a form or its instructions must be retained as long as their contents may become material in the administration of any Internal Revenue law. Generally, tax returns and return information are confidential, as required by Code section 6103. Although the time needed to complete this form may vary depending on individual circumstances, the estimated average time is 30 minutes. Should you have comments concerning the accuracy of this time estimate or suggestions for making this form simpler, please write to the Internal Revenue Service, Attention: Tax Forms Committee, Western Area Distribution Center, Rancho Cordova, CA 95743-0001.

Cat. No. 16965S　　　　　　　　　　　　　　　　　　　　　　　　　　　　　　　　Form **911** (Rev. 3-2000)

Where to File Your Request

It is important that you file your request using the address shown on your lien or levy notice. If you have been working with a specific IRS employee on your case, you should file the request with that employee.

How to Complete Form 12153

1. Enter your full name and address. If the tax liability is owed jointly by a husband and wife, and both wish to request a Collection Due Process Hearing, show both names.

2. Enter a daytime telephone number where we can contact you regarding your request for a hearing.

3. List the type(s) of tax or the number of the tax form(s) for which you are requesting a hearing (e.g. Form 1040, Form 941, Trust Fund Recovery Penalty, etc.).

4. List the taxable periods for the type(s) of tax or the tax form(s) that you listed for item 3 above (e.g., year ending 12-31-98, quarter ending 3-31-98).

5. Show the social security number of the individual(s) and/or the employer identification number of the business(s) that are requesting a hearing.

6. Check the IRS action(s) that you do not agree with (Filed Notice of Federal Tax Lien and/or Notice of Levy/Seizure). You may check both actions if applicable.

7. Provide the specific reason(s) why you do not agree with the filing of the Notice of Federal Tax Lien or the proposed Notice of Levy/Seizure action. One specific issue that you may raise at the hearing is whether income taxes should be abated because you believe that your spouse or former spouse should be responsible for all or a portion of the tax liability from your tax return. You must, however, elect such relief. You can do this by checking the indicated box and attaching Form 8857 to this request for a hearing. If you previously filed Form 8857, please indicate when and with whom you filed the Form.

8. You, or your authorized representative, must sign the Form 12153. If the tax liability is joint and both spouses are requesting a hearing, both spouses, or their authorized representative(s), must sign.

9. It is important that you understand that we are required by statute to suspend the statutory period for collection during a Collection Due Process Hearing.

Request for a Collection Due Process Hearing

Use this form to request a hearing with the IRS Office of Appeals only when you receive a **Notice of Federal Tax Lien Filing & Your Right To A Hearing Under IRC 6320**, a **Final Notice - Notice Of Intent to Levy & Your Notice Of a Right To A Hearing**, or a **Notice of Jeopardy Levy and Right of Appeal**. Complete this form and send it to the address shown on your lien or levy notice for expeditious handling. Include a copy of your lien or levy notice(s) to ensure proper handling of your request.

(Print) Taxpayer Name(s):_____

(Print) Address: _____

Daytime Telephone Number:_____ Type of Tax/Tax Form Number(s):_____

Taxable Period(s):_____

Social Security Number/Employer Identification Number(s):_____

Check the IRS action(s) that you do not agree with. Provide specific reasons why you don't agree. If you believe that your spouse or former spouse should be responsible for all or a portion of the tax liability from your tax return, check here [__] and attach Form 8857, Request for Innocent Spouse Relief, to this request.

_____ **Filed Notice of Federal Tax Lien (Explain why you don't agree. Use extra sheets if necessary.)**

_____ **Notice of Levy/Seizure (Explain why you don't agree. Use extra sheets if necessary.)**

I/we understand that the statutory period of limitations for collection is suspended during the Collection Due Process Hearing and any subsequent judicial review.

Taxpayer's or Authorized Representative's Signature and Date:_____

Taxpayer's or Authorized Representative's Signature and Date:_____

IRS Use Only:

IRS Employee *(Print)*: _____ IRS Received Date:_____

Employee Telephone Number: _____

Form **12153** (01-1999)   Catalog Number 26685D   **(Over)**   Department of the Treasury -- Internal Revenue Service

Form **2848**
(Rev. January 2002)
Department of the Treasury
Internal Revenue Service

Power of Attorney and Declaration of Representative

▶ See the separate instructions.

OMB No. 1545-0150

For IRS Use Only
Received by:
Name
Telephone
Function
Date / /

Part I Power of Attorney (Type or print.)

1 Taxpayer information. Taxpayer(s) must sign and date this form on page 2, line 9.

Taxpayer name(s) and address	Social security number(s)	Employer identification number
	Daytime telephone number ( )	Plan number (if applicable)

hereby appoint(s) the following representative(s) as attorney(s)-in-fact:

2 Representative(s) must sign and date this form on page 2, Part II.

Name and address	CAF No. .... Telephone No. .... Fax No. .... Check if new: Address ☐ Telephone No. ☐
Name and address	CAF No. .... Telephone No. .... Fax No. .... Check if new: Address ☐ Telephone No. ☐
Name and address	CAF No. .... Telephone No. .... Fax No. .... Check if new: Address ☐ Telephone No. ☐

to represent the taxpayer(s) before the Internal Revenue Service for the following tax matters:

3 Tax matters

Type of Tax (Income, Employment, Excise, etc.) or Civil Penalty (See the instructions for line 3.)	Tax Form Number (1040, 941, 720, etc.)	Year(s) or Period(s)

4 Specific use not recorded on Centralized Authorization File (CAF). If the power of attorney is for a specific use not recorded on CAF, check this box. See the instructions for **Line 4. Specific uses not recorded on CAF.** . . . . ▶ ☐

5 Acts authorized. The representatives are authorized to receive and inspect confidential tax information and to perform any and all acts that I (we) can perform with respect to the tax matters described on line 3, for example, the authority to sign any agreements, consents, or other documents. The authority does not include the power to receive refund checks (see line 6 below), the power to substitute another representative, the authority to execute a request for a tax return, or a consent to disclose tax information unless specifically added below, or the power to sign certain returns. See the instructions for **Line 5. Acts authorized.**

List any specific additions or deletions to the acts otherwise authorized in this power of attorney: ....
....

Note: *In general, an unenrolled preparer of tax returns cannot sign any document for a taxpayer. See Revenue Procedure 81-38, printed as Pub. 470, for more information.*

Note: *The tax matters partner of a partnership is not permitted to authorize representatives to perform certain acts. See the separate instructions for more information.*

6 Receipt of refund checks. If you want to authorize a representative named on line 2 to receive, **BUT NOT TO ENDORSE OR CASH,** refund checks, initial here _____ and list the name of that representative below.

Name of representative to receive refund check(s) ▶

For Paperwork Reduction and Privacy Act Notice, see the separate instructions. Cat. No. 11980J Form **2848** (Rev. 1-2002)

Form 2848 (Rev. 1-2002) Page **2**

7 Notices and communications. Original notices and other written communications will be sent to you and a copy to the first representative listed on line 2 unless you check one or more of the boxes below.
  a If you want the first representative listed on line 2 to receive the original, and yourself a copy, of such notices or communications, check this box . . . . ▶ ☐
  b If you also want the second representative listed to receive a copy of such notices and communications, check this box. ▶ ☐
  c If you do not want any notices or communications sent to your representative(s), check this box . . . . . . ▶ ☐

8 Retention/revocation of prior power(s) of attorney. The filing of this power of attorney automatically revokes all earlier power(s) of attorney on file with the Internal Revenue Service for the same tax matters and years or periods covered by this document. If you **do not** want to revoke a prior power of attorney, check here . . . . ▶ ☐
  YOU MUST ATTACH A COPY OF ANY POWER OF ATTORNEY YOU WANT TO REMAIN IN EFFECT.

9 Signature of taxpayer(s). If a tax matter concerns a joint return, **both** husband and wife must sign if joint representation is requested, otherwise, see the instructions. If signed by a corporate officer, partner, guardian, tax matters partner, executor, receiver, administrator, or trustee on behalf of the taxpayer, I certify that I have the authority to execute this form on behalf of the taxpayer.

▶ **IF NOT SIGNED AND DATED, THIS POWER OF ATTORNEY WILL BE RETURNED.**

_____   _____   _____
Signature   Date   Title (if applicable)

_____
Print Name

_____   _____   _____
Signature   Date   Title (if applicable)

_____
Print Name

Part II Declaration of Representative

Caution: *Students with a special order to represent taxpayers in Qualified Low Income Taxpayer Clinics or the Student Tax Clinic Program, see the separate instructions for Part II.*

Under penalties of perjury, I declare that:
- I am not currently under suspension or disbarment from practice before the Internal Revenue Service;
- I am aware of regulations contained in Treasury Department Circular No. 230 (31 CFR, Part 10), as amended, concerning the practice of attorneys, certified public accountants, enrolled agents, enrolled actuaries, and others;
- I am authorized to represent the taxpayer(s) identified in Part I for the tax matter(s) specified there; and
- I am one of the following:
  a Attorney- a member in good standing of the bar of the highest court of the jurisdiction shown below.
  b Certified Public Accountant- duly qualified to practice as a certified public accountant in the jurisdiction shown below.
  c Enrolled Agent- enrolled as an agent under the requirements of Treasury Department Circular No. 230.
  d Officer- a bona fide officer of the taxpayer's organization.
  e Full-Time Employee- a full-time employee of the taxpayer.
  f Family Member- a member of the taxpayer's immediate family (i.e., spouse, parent, child, brother, or sister).
  g Enrolled Actuary- enrolled as an actuary by the Joint Board for the Enrollment of Actuaries under 29 U.S.C. 1242 (the authority to practice before the Service is limited by section 10.3(d)(1) of Treasury Department Circular No. 230).
  h Unenrolled Return Preparer- an unenrolled return preparer under section 10.7(c)(1)(viii) of Treasury Department Circular No. 230.

▶ **IF THIS DECLARATION OF REPRESENTATIVE IS NOT SIGNED AND DATED, THE POWER OF ATTORNEY WILL BE RETURNED.**

Designation- Insert above letter (a- h)	Jurisdiction (state) or Enrollment Card No.	Signature	Date

Form **2848** (Rev. 1-2002)

0-595-31683-2

Printed in the United States
83729LV00005B/106-108/A